BOLDLY INTO THE DARKNESS

BOLDLY INTO THE DARKNESS

LIVING with LOSS, GROWING with GRIEF & HOLDING on to HAPPINESS

AUTUMN TOELLE-JACKSON

WISE INK

Minneapolis

ISBN 13: 978-1-63489-357-2

Library of Congress Catalog Number: 2020912030
Printed in the United States of America
First Printing: 2021

25   24   23   22   21   5   4   3   2   1

Cover design by Steve Meyer-Rassow
Interior design by Patrick Maloney

Wise Ink Creative Publishing
807 Broadway St NE
Suite 46
Minneapolis, MN, 55413

To order, visit www.GrowingWithGrief.com

This book is dedicated to those I have lost:

Joe, the love of my first life, who brought me happiness both while alive and with memories after death.

Brittany, a cousin who was more like a sister, and the person I always looked up to and wanted to be like.

Rylee, our beautiful daughter, a gift in my second life who left us too soon but whose smile and bright eyes will always be a treasure to my heart.

And to those I'm lucky enough to still hold on to in this world:

Cody, my oldest son, who makes me proud with his intellect and compassion.

Wade, my youngest son, who warms me with his sense of humor and lightheartedness.

Kyle, the love of my second life and my biggest supporter, who helped me navigate my darkness and grab happiness; who willingly embraced me, my sons, my family, and Joe's family, and claimed us all as his own.

I love you.

"Owning our story can be hard but not nearly as difficult as spending our lives running from it. Embracing our vulnerabilities is risky but not nearly as dangerous as giving up on love and belonging and joy—the experiences that make us the most vulnerable. Only when we are brave enough to explore the darkness will we discover the infinite power of our light."

—Brené Brown,
The Gifts of Imperfection

I am not the first person you loved.
You are not the first person I looked at
with a mouthful of forevers. We
have both known loss like the sharp edges
of a knife. We have both lived with lips
more scar tissue than skin. Our love came
unannounced in the middle of the night.
Our love came when we'd given up
on asking love to come. I think
that has to be part
of its miracle.

This is how we heal.
I will kiss you like forgiveness. You
will hold me like I'm hope. Our arms
will bandage and we will press promises
between us like flowers in a book.
I will write sonnets to the salt of sweat
on your skin. I will write novels to the scar
of your nose. I will write a dictionary
of all the words I have used trying
to describe the way it feels to have finally,
finally found you.

And I will not be afraid
of your scars.

I know sometimes
it's still hard to let me see you

in all your cracked perfection,
but please know:
whether it's the days you burn
more brilliant than the sun
or the nights you collapse into my lap
your body broken into a thousand questions,
you are the most beautiful thing I've ever seen.
I will love you when you are a still day.
I will love you when you are a hurricane.

—Clementine von Radics, "Mouthful of Forevers"

Introduction

I F THE BIG EVENTS IN my life were placed on a timeline, that timeline would have a happily ordinary start, resembling the life of someone who grew up in the middle class. I'd appear as someone who hadn't faced hardships or dealt with loss, barring that of an occasional pet and some of my grandparents. That changed later in my life. My first real hardship occurred when I was thirty years old and experienced miscarriages. And over the next few years, I'd lose a husband, a close family member, and a child.

It's a pattern of love and loss, with the losses dominating. But a timeline doesn't explain life. When you know only the big events, it's easy to think, "How sad and horrible, so much loss," or, "Wow, her life sucks." Except it doesn't. A timeline shows only the big events, not the life that's lived in between, the parts that connect happy and sad or smiles and tears. A timeline doesn't show the continued struggles, nor does it show the many smaller blessings. It doesn't show fear or hope. It doesn't show the story, and the story is what matters.

Between the covers of this book, you'll find a story. It's not an exciting story full of fun and adventure. It's not a comedy filled with jokes and laughter. There's no monster to fight; and despite traumatic events, it's not a traumatic story. Instead, it's a story overflowing with love and marked with loss. A story of rebirth and resilience, strength and hope, pain and darkness. It's a story of life—my story. It's written how I remember it, often clouded by the shock of grief. Even with all the trauma and death, my life has been blessed.

It was often hard to see that blessedness, though. It was hard to see the good when my world was suddenly and repeatedly thrust into the darkness. I struggled to breathe and survive, even when I knew I wanted something more than the struggle, more than the grief I'd carry with me. Through my story, I began to grasp at rays of light that would break through, small pieces of hope that let me rebuild myself into something strong enough to withstand the weight of this new life.

Over time, I learned that, with each new grief, I'd shatter and then find a way to survive, whether I wanted to or not. I learned that I had choices, and I've chosen to do more than live. I learned that while the darkness brought sobs of anguish and never-ending tears, it also held healing and rebirth. I learned to live with my losses. I found ways to grow from the grief I carry. Most importantly, I learned to grab hope wherever I could find it and hold on tight, because sometimes the hope that things will get better was all I had. Those we lose are more than the loss. They are love, laughter, and happiness. That should be their legacy. Their death shouldn't define them. Our loved ones are more than that one point in time.

Yes, my life has sad and horrible parts, but it also has so many more wonderful parts. Yes, I lost, but I have loved and been loved. I've chosen to do more than just survive. I chose to be more than a victim of my circumstances. I've chosen to share my story, in this book and in my life, because I want others to see that it's possible to live and grow with grief. It's possible to go boldly into the darkness and come out stronger and more beautiful, not in spite of being broken but because of being broken. More than that, I want to share hope. I want to give others that small piece of hope that others gave me when my world was at its darkest.

As horrible as life can be, we were made to survive it. I hope as you read my story, you can find your own strength to live your life as it was meant to be lived: with hope, laughter, and love.

I

D O YOU HAVE A SANCTUARY? A place where you can go and feel safe? A place where, no matter what else is going on in the world, you feel at peace the moment you enter it? For Joe, my first husband, this was the ranch.

The ranch is located twenty miles east of Burns, Oregon. Joe's grandparents had purchased the ranch and moved their family there when their children were young. While Joe didn't live at the ranch, it was in his blood. He took me to the ranch the first time I visited him in Burns.

The long driveway curved along the base of a hill, traveling into a canyon. Cow Creek meandered through the meadows on the other side, where the green grass waved in the wind. My first glimpse of the ranch was a cluster of old trees situated in the mouth of the canyon.

As we got closer, I was able to pick out details. Farm equipment was parked in orderly rows, waiting to be used. Cows were grazing on the sagebrush-covered hillsides. The trees separated into weeping willows, birches with bright white bark, apple trees, pear trees, and a large lawn surrounding the ranch house. As we turned into the yard, I was greeted by the sight of an old red barn with horses in the corrals behind it. Curly, Blue, and Lucy, the three ranch dogs, ran to meet us.

Joe didn't have to tell me what the ranch meant to him. I could see it in the way he smiled as he showed me around, with pride shining in his brown eyes. Joe may not have lived at the ranch, but it was clear he belonged there. The respectful way he treated me, opening doors and guiding me with a gentle touch to the small of my back; his love of cows, dogs, horses, and other animals; his ability to rope and ride—he learned all those things and more under the shadows of those trees.

Once we finished college and were married, there was no question we would settle in Burns. Joe needed to be near that ranch. The thought of living anywhere else wasn't something he was willing to consider.

Growing up on the ranch also led to Joe's passion for hunting. He would spend hours talking with people about different places to go, strategies, gear, or just sharing stories. It was a frequent topic of Joe's conversations, no matter if he had known the person he was talking to for years or minutes. I didn't hunt with him, partly because I didn't care to hunt. The one time I did go, it was impossible for me to keep up with him and his long strides. When he would hunt locally, he would just walk and walk and walk. Ten or twenty miles a day. So when I slowed him down, it forced him to choose between holding back for me or going after his target. Let's just say he hesitated making a decision and ended up not dissatisfied with the result.

Joe loved hunting elk, though mule deer was his favorite. He liked the challenge of it and the chance to provide meat for the family. He was open to new hunting experiences too, and was stoked when a friend invited him to go caribou hunting in Alaska in August 2015. After that, he spent hours online, researching the best gear and trying to figure out how to maximize the equipment he could bring with him without going over the maximum weight each person was allowed to bring on the plane. He made an Excel spreadsheet to keep track of each piece of gear and what it would weigh, organizing it by needed gear, and then created different scenarios to help him determine what other equipment he should bring and what he would have to leave home.

In addition to making his lists, Joe started working out. It wasn't like he was in bad shape. He was six foot three and usually weighed around 210 pounds. He had also spent eleven years as a wildland firefighter and, despite working the last two years as an engineer, still worked as a firefighter on evenings and weekends when he could. He had the annual physicals required for firefighters, and despite eating a lot of food, wasn't overweight. But for Alaska, he wanted to be in the best shape possible. He wanted to be able to do whatever he needed while he was there without getting too sore or worn out.

For his workout routine, Joe would jog and play men's league basketball a few nights each week. On some nights, he would do both. Luckily, the winter of 2014 and 2015 was mild, and Joe was able to keep working out outside. He took a short break when our youngest son, Wade, was born, but he was back at it after that first week. He would go for a run in the evenings when I was feeding Wade and after he played with our oldest son, Cody, and put him into bed. On the nights he had basketball, he would go running afterward if the weather let him, even though it was late. That was what happened on February 5, 2015.

THAT DAY WAS LIKE any other day in our lives. Family who had been visiting after Wade was born had finally left, and it was just the four of us getting into a routine. Joe had just gone back to work after taking a week off; and that morning, after giving me and Wade goodbye kisses, he took Cody to daycare and went to work while I stayed home with Wade. After work, Joe came home and we had dinner. He then spent time with both of our sons and put them to bed before getting ready to go play basketball.

Before Joe left that evening, he told me he was going to jog after basketball, but that he wasn't going to come into the house because he didn't want to wake us up if we were sleeping. He gave me a kiss, told me he loved us, jumped into his truck, and left.

Around ten o'clock, I heard Joe's truck pull up. I was getting ready to feed Wade, and I knew Joe would go for a jog. So I didn't get up to meet him at the door. Normally, he would jog for about thirty to forty-five minutes. But as I finished feeding Wade and put him to sleep, a cold wave of fear came over me. Something was wrong. I looked at the clock.

It was 10:45 p.m. Where was Joe? He should have been back by then.

While my heart was telling me to panic, my head was telling me he had probably hurt his ankle or knee. After all, he was just getting back to jogging. And knowing him, he wasn't jogging in his tennis shoes. He had to keep those nice for the gym, so he was jogging in his slip-on shoes. He was just hurt; I was sure of it.

I placed Wade in the bassinet by our bed and put on a coat. It was the beginning of February in eastern Oregon, and warm was still relative. Then I jumped into my car. It hadn't crossed my mind to put on something more or to grab my phone. I thought I wouldn't need it, that we'd be right back and I could change if we needed to go to the hospital, which I didn't think was likely. Joe had once been run over by a fire truck that weighed over twenty thousand pounds, then spent the night at fire camp before going to the hospital the next morning. Once he was there, the doctors found he had no broken bones or major issues, just some swelling and a tire track bruise from his knee to his ankle.

In Joe's own mind, he was invincible. After all, his

eighty-five-year-old grandpa was a former rodeo cowboy and rancher who still rode horses, roped at brandings, and did better than most men no matter their age. Joe had told a friend not long before that he had good genetics and would probably live to be at least ninety, and he believed it with all his heart. I tried to convince myself Joe was slowly gimping home, and I just needed to find him and give him a ride. The thought that it would be worse hadn't occurred to me.

I paused for a minute at the end of our driveway, trying to decide which way to go. It was dark, and the road we lived on had no streetlights, though the moon and stars made it somewhat easier to see. Eventually I turned right, because when Joe had first started running, that was the way he had gone. From there, if he had run all the way to the barrier gate and back, it was almost three miles.

I drove to the gate, but I didn't see Joe. So I hurried back, straining to see down the road, hoping I'd see him jogging toward me. When I came back to the house, I ran in just to make sure he hadn't gotten home while I was away. But Joe was still missing.

A ball of energy formed in the pit of my stomach. I started to panic. It was like my body had gathered all my energy and emotions and trapped them in my stomach, pulling more and more from my body. In my mind, the ball was a cold, electric blue, and its center tightened and became dense with each new piece wrapping around it, the ends loose and waving. As these ends waved around, they touched parts of me, jolting me with a sharp, tingly, numbing feeling that spread throughout the rest of my body. The jolts felt warm, though they didn't warm my body. In fact, I felt my body get colder, and I started to shiver.

I wasn't familiar with the feeling at the time. Today, however, I'm sure it was the feeling of extreme stress on my body, the release of hormones meant to jolt my body into action. I associate these feelings with shock. It's my mind's way of trying to protect my body. But that night, I didn't know any of this. I just knew it meant something was very wrong.

Joe wasn't home. That was wrong, and I knew the reason he wasn't home was even more wrong.

I ran back outside to the car, aware that the quiet in the house suggested the boys were still sleeping, and turned left out of our driveway. There were no sounds in the night other than my short, panicked breaths. I scanned the dark road, picking out the neighbors' mailboxes and looking for someone walking—or, more likely, limping—home. It wasn't until I was less than fifty feet away that I noticed the dark shape of someone lying on the side of the road.

I slammed on the brakes and stopped the car in the middle of the road, not caring if it was in someone's way. I ran out to Joe, still trying to understand what I was seeing but unable to do so. This was just some elaborate joke he had come up with to freak me out. It didn't matter that he had never played a prank like this on me before. That must be it; it wasn't real. As soon as I talked to him, he would sit up and give me a hug and say he was sorry for scaring me.

But I didn't get to hold on to that dream for long. Once I was at his side, I realized Joe was lying on his back in the gravel on the shoulder of the road. Everything was still. Too still, like the stillness that comes over a forest when a predator is near.

I knelt beside him and grabbed his warm hands. Called his name, then yelled it, then screamed it. I checked to see if he was breathing, if he had a pulse. Years of first aid and CPR training were trying to surface. I slapped his face—not hard, but enough to try to jolt him awake. I cursed myself for not having a phone. I screamed for someone to help. I ran to my car and honked my horn, trying to wake someone up and get help in our rural neighborhood.

I have no idea how much time passed. It seemed like an eternity as I prayed to God for help and yelled at Joe, telling him he couldn't do this to me, telling myself this wasn't real, it couldn't be happening, it must be a bad dream. But I didn't wake up.

About a minute later, I realized I needed to get someone to call 911. This meant I had to leave Joe. So I jumped back into my car and drove down the nearest driveway. I knew who lived there; the man was my boss, and his wife had been friends with Joe's mom for years. I skidded to a stop and ran into their garage and then the house, screaming for them to call 911, that I had found Joe and he was on the side of the road. I had never been in their house before; I didn't know where to go, and I had hesitated about bursting into someone else's house. The manners I had been raised with were in the back of my mind but were quickly overruled by my need for help.

As soon as I heard my boss and his wife respond, trying to ask me questions, I yelled again for them to call 911, ran back to the car, and drove back to Joe, parking in the middle of the road so the headlights were shining on him. Then I started CPR. I focused on compressions and was soon joined by my boss, and we worked on Joe as a team. My boss asked me what happened; I screamed that I didn't know, that this couldn't be happening, that it wasn't real and Joe couldn't leave me. I kept asking questions that had no answers. How could this be happening? Why?

My boss's wife came out then. She knelt down by Joe's feet and told me she had called 911 and the ambulance was on its way. I kept asking her where they were and saw tears on her face as she told me she didn't know but that they were coming. I continued to pump Joe's chest, hoping to save him, straining to hear a siren. The fact that we lived about three miles outside of town and that it was a process to dispatch the EMTs on call in our small rural community didn't register with me. And it didn't matter. Only the fact that it was taking too long mattered. It seemed like hours as I kept doing chest compressions, hoping Joe's blood was circulating.

A sheriff's deputy arrived about fifteen minutes later (though it may have been more like five minutes). He and Joe had gone to school together, and his wife worked at the same place as me and Joe. The deputy gently looked at what was going on and asked me to step aside, saying that he would do compressions until the ambulance got there. As I stood there at eleven-something at night, watching them try to save Joe, I finally had a chance to look at him. He was just lying there, with no wounds I could see. His legs were straight, and his arms were out to the side, a few inches from his body, hands open and relaxed. His eyes were mostly closed, but not quite. I could still see them a little, a warm brown color that lacked the spark that the soul provides—the spark that's present with life.

That was the point when I realized Joe was already gone—and he must have died quickly.

As I stood there alone, I truly felt the emptiness that was now my life. Or maybe it was the emptiness of my metaphorical death: the death of my life as I had known it, and of the future I had planned. I'd always felt Joe when I was near him, felt him in my heart and soul, even when we weren't right next to each other or touching. I had felt his presence and it had warmed me since the first time I saw him. Now, a coldness seeped into my body. I felt like I had entered a fog, with thick gray mist settling around me, blocking out the stars and dulling all noise. A threat was lurking there: the threat of love lost, a grief I didn't yet know was possible. I couldn't see it, but I could feel it circling me in the fog that filled my soul.

As I watched the deputy and my boss continue to perform CPR

on Joe, I realized I needed to call people. My fog and the threat I felt were mine alone. But I knew other people shared my love for Joe, and they deserved to know that something was wrong.

My boss's wife brought me my phone, and I called Joe's brother first, then his dad, his mom, my parents, my sister, and finally some of Joe's best friends. I don't remember much about the calls. The calls were probably less than coherent, and I got frustrated after a while because no one was answering right away. But eventually I got ahold of most of them.

Joe's brother lived in our town. He had seen Joe just a few hours earlier as they were playing basketball, and Joe had appeared to be in perfect health. He hurried over as soon as I told him what had happened. His dad and his grandpa, who lived at the ranch about twenty minutes from town, also jumped in their trucks and came over.

When I finally reached Joe's mom, I told her he had gone jogging and I had found him collapsed on the side of the road, and that they were performing CPR on him but it didn't look good. Her cries of anguish matched the ones I was feeling in my body. She asked me what had happened, but I wasn't able to answer her. I can't imagine the feeling of helplessness as a parent, to be so far away, in a different state, and know your child is in danger—or, even worse, dead. The helplessness I felt was bad enough.

Eventually the ambulance came, and the EMTs took over on CPR. I have no idea how long they worked on him. I could look it up; I have all the records. But it doesn't matter now. It seemed like they worked on him for an eternity.

When Joe's brother got there, he looked at Joe, who was still receiving CPR, and then came to me. We stood there hugging, trying to hold each other up as we both lost our best friend. We cried together and waited.

I stood there on the side of the road with Joe's brother and my boss, with lights from the ambulance and police cars flashing around us. I prayed and hoped and cried. I waited for them to load him up and take him to the hospital. But then the EMTs stopped working on him and slowly stood up. The sheriff's deputy who had first arrived on the scene slowly walked over to me. I thought I saw tears in his eyes, but I clearly saw pain on his face.

"They stopped working on him," I said in a voice that sounded dead and unfamiliar, lacking emotion. "That's not good, is it?"

The sheriff's deputy didn't have to say much. In my mind, he said, "No. I'm sorry." But by that point, the fog had set in, and my memory of that moment is filled with haze and gaps. Whatever the deputy said didn't matter. Nothing did.

Joe's dad arrived after they stopped working on Joe. I can't remember what actually happened then. In my fragmented memories, I see Joe's dad hugging his son on the ground. He didn't say anything when he came over and hugged me. No words were needed. Loss is a concept that's too difficult to truly grasp until you live through it. Nothing would make this OK or better, and nothing would comfort us. Joe—a son, a brother, a husband, a father, and a friend to many—was gone.

And the person I had been, along with all my hopes, dreams, plans, and goals, died with him on the side of that road. There was no going back.

I have no idea how long we stood there before a state police officer came over and suggested we go back to the house—*my* house. There was no longer an *our* in my life. Before I did, though, I thanked the EMTs and everyone who had come to help. After all, it was a small town; and many of the first responders either knew Joe personally, knew of him, or knew of his family. First responders in rural communities get a shitty deal. They rarely have the luxury of not knowing who they are working on—who they save or who they lose. I had no idea what had happened or why my husband was dead on the side of the road, but I knew without a doubt that everyone had tried their hardest to save him. Even if my brain was unable to grasp that through the fog, my heart was able to see it. I went to each person, thanking them for their help, and saw the tears glistening in their eyes and on their cheeks as they offered me their condolences, the only thing they had left to give.

Back at the house, I was so confused, unable to fully grasp what had just happened. A healthy thirty-year-old man doesn't just die, especially not right after we had a baby, not when our life was so perfect. I sat in Joe's recliner and stared into the darkness that was enveloping me.

At one point, police officers came and said they were sorry, that they had a few questions but could come back later. I told them no, that I wanted to go through it all right now or as soon as possible. They told me that it might have been a hit-and-run, and said the ambulance had taken Joe's body to the hospital to look for any sign of injury. Then they were gone; and I was still sitting there, alone in a house slowly filling with people and trying to remember who I needed to call, text, or somehow inform personally, because the whole county would know come morning.

Word of mouth is still a main source of information in rural communities. So I needed to let the other people who were important to Joe know that he had died before they saw the horrible truth on Facebook or heard it from a neighbor. In my mind, I had to be the person to let his other friends know. I never even considered that using a text to tell someone their friend was dead wasn't in good taste. It just seemed easier.

Months later, I found out I had left out one good friend on

that text. She found out while working in the hospital's account-
ing department the morning after Joe died, when someone asked
her how to bill for tests on a patient who was dead on arrival. I
can't imagine the shock she must have felt when she heard the
patient's name. I wish I had remembered to send her that text. I
did the best I could in letting people know, and yet I still feel like
I failed her.

Surprisingly, even as I was forced deep into the darkness and
was unable to see a glimmer of light around me, I was still able to
function that night. Not fully and not well, but I could do what
I needed to do. I did it blindly and without much thought, but I
could still do it. This included telling my son Cody, who was almost
three years old, that his dad was dead. Not that we'd lost him or that
he was gone, but that he was dead. That his heart had stopped and
we would never again see him. That we would have to remember
him and love him, but that he was never coming home again. The
man who made Cody laugh, whom Cody always begged to make
the truck "go faster," and whom Cody asked for constantly when he
was hunting or at work, was no longer alive.

And I'd have to tell Cody alone. Because I was alone now. It
was my job, alone, to take care of our kids.

I don't remember that conversation. But I do know that I wondered, How do I do this? How can I do this alone, without Joe?
He's supposed to be there to help me with hard situations. How
do I shatter this little boy's world? How do I make sure he survives
this loss when I don't feel like I can?

I knew I needed to do it soon, before Cody realized all his
family wasn't there for fun. I wish I could tell you what I did and
what I said, but I can't. I think I went into his room alone when
he woke up and told him, but my mom might have been there as

well. All I do remember is that he looked at me with his blue-gray eyes, and I wondered how much he understood.

I don't remember Cody crying or sobbing. Perhaps he did, and I was unable to recognize it through my own tears. But what I do know is he never asked for his dad again; and I don't know how it was possible, but my heart broke even more.

2

GROWING UP, I KNEW I was pretty lucky. My parents worked hard, but they knew how important it was to have fun. All five of us—me, my parents, my brother, and my sister—would do things with my aunt, uncle, and two cousins. And when I say *things*, I mean pretty much everything. These relatives lived in Springfield, a town near Eugene, Oregon, so we didn't see them all the time. But we spent every major holiday—Christmas, Thanksgiving, and Easter—and almost all our trips with them. Plus, we would always stay at least one full week each summer at their house. One of my cousins was my sister's age, about four years older than me. The other cousin, Brittany, was two years older than me and the one I connected with most.

Brittany took the time to play and talk with me. She taught me how to make jewelry out of beads and how to ride a horse. She was my role model. I took my cues in life from her, and her loves became my loves, whether it was for horses, dogs, music, or other things. With Brittany, life was simple, happy, and full.

My first real loss was when we had to give away our German shepherd, Pedro. This was followed by other pets. Then, when I was ten, my seventy-nine-year-old paternal grandfather died, followed by my eighty-six-year-old great-grandmother when I was thirteen. I heard my parents talk from time to time about them being sick, but both my grandfather and great-grandmother were old and lived in other towns. When they died, it was sad, and I missed them. But more than that, I felt bad that my parents were sad.

Sure, I'd miss the trips to my grandpa's, where he would let us "play" with his model trains under his close supervision, swim in the creek, and pick blackberries. And I'd remember the life lessons my great-grandma taught me, like how to use her wheelchair to take turns going down the ramp in the mall; how to play cards, especially poker, the proper way; and how your bra was the perfect place to keep your tissues. But they died, and that was what happened; people died when they were old. At least, that was what I thought back then.

Even though I was old enough to remember their memorial services, my memories of both events are limited. At my grandfather's service, I knelt down on the little bench that tips down from the pew in front of you. Being nondenominational Christians, our family didn't have them at our church; and I spent a lot of time admiring them and wondering why people would go to a church that required them to kneel so often that they needed a cushion for comfort. At my great-grandma's service, I saw my great-grandma lying in the open casket, and it traumatized me—not because I had seen a dead person, but because I didn't recognize the woman I had seen in the coffin. Sickness had stolen the large, boisterous, hearty woman in bright pink lipstick and replaced her with a tiny old lady I could have snapped in half if I hugged her.

Otherwise, that was my experience with loss as a young girl: pets, a great-grandma, and a grandpa.

Except for those few sad interruptions, my life as a middle-class Caucasian girl growing up in a small Oregon city was pretty normal. I followed in Brittany's footsteps and got a horse, then began competing with it when I was eight years old. That continued to be my main focus through high school. Brittany set a high standard, and to even come close to competing at that level, I needed to focus, practice, and grow. This was even more true when I purchased Brittany's horse, Norman, after she graduated from high school. I knew that even with her horse, I'd never be able to fill her shoes. But I wanted to do my best, make Brittany proud, and not give her any reason for regretting passing Norman on to me.

BETWEEN THAT AND SCHOOL, I had very little time to do much else. This included going on dates, which limited my number of high school relationships to two. One was due to boredom in a few moments of downtime, when we were both in the same place and the same time. The other was during my senior year and ended with the stereotypical high schooler's broken heart.

After high school, I went to the University of Idaho. I wasn't competing with my horse as much and had time to date, but I was gun-shy and introverted. I made friends and had some opportunities, but nothing ever felt right or worth the loss of my alone time. Even though the University of Idaho, which is located in Moscow, Idaho, was more than six hours north of Bend, Oregon, where my family still lived, I preferred to drive back home on a weekend and compete with Norman or stay in and read a good book rather than go out and party. I would go out occasionally, if for no reason other than to humor my friends. But my college experience was pretty boring yet immensely satisfying. After all, for the first time, I was in charge of myself and got to make all my own choices.

When I was twenty, my old high school boyfriend invited me to his wedding. We had remained friends, though I'm not sure why his fiancée had agreed to invite me. I drove to Bend and convinced my best friend to go with me and make me presentable. I had never really mastered the typical feminine skills of doing hair and makeup. But for some reason, I felt like I needed to look extra good that night. My dress was light blue with a simple halter top and wraparound skirt that was short in the front and longer in the back. It wasn't flashy, but for me the beaded flowers around the skirt were extra feminine; and I felt confident, ready to take on the world in a dress and high heels rather than my standard blue jeans and cowboy boots.

I first saw Joe while we were waiting for the ceremony to start, though I didn't learn his name until later that night. He was tall and dark with soft brown eyes and a slight goatee; and he was wearing a nice button-up shirt, blue Wranglers, cowboy boots, and a University of North Carolina baseball hat. I had no idea who he was, but from the moment I saw him, I had trouble seeing anything else. I'm sure the ceremony was everything it should have been, but I spent most of the time trying to get another look at him through the rows of heads between us.

At the reception later on, my attention was drawn to him. I watched him slip away to the back room with a girl every so often and felt jealous, then lectured myself about that jealousy. I had no idea who this man was. I thought I was being subtle, but my friend pointed out that anyone who paid attention to me for more than two minutes would be able to tell I was distracted and could follow my gaze to find the reason why. Eventually my friend left out of boredom; and I stayed with other friends, unwilling to pry myself away from this stranger who had enthralled me in a way no one, and nothing, ever had.

Because I was shy, quiet, and happily sitting against the wall away from the activities, I had no intention or thought of approaching this man. However, I needed him to be a part of my life a little longer. As the night went on and the crowd thinned, my presence along the wall became more noticeable. The bride came over to try to convince me to dance—something I tried to avoid at all costs, since it put me out in the open more than I preferred and I had less rhythm than a two-year-old. But then the bride suggested I dance with Joe and pointed him out. Finally I had a name for my infatuation. Despite my desire not to dance, and thanks to my not-so-subtle spying, I had just heard him turn down a dance from another girl. I was unwilling to risk that. Eventually the bride and groom wore us both down, and we ended up dancing with some members from the wedding party. We weren't dancing with each other, but for that entire song, as we danced with other people, we looked at each other.

I'm not sure if that was when Joe first noticed me, or if he had noticed me earlier. But during that first forced dance with strangers, it was obvious that we both felt drawn to each other. There was no awkwardness and no attempt to hide it. We stared at each other enough that both of our partners noticed and were more than a little annoyed by the end of the song. Then Joe and I danced together and talked the rest of the night.

I found out he was nineteen and attending the Oregon Institute of Technology in Klamath Falls, about two hours south of Bend. He was getting a degree in mechanical engineering despite wanting to stay at home in Burns and help his dad and granddad run the family ranch. (Going to college was nonnegotiable, in his dad's opinion.) He was a wildland firefighter during the summers, and he had "dated" the bride during high school. They had recently reconnected, and he had found himself with an invitation to the wedding, which he decided to attend since he had bought a car a few weeks earlier and could make the drive without it bankrupting him like his truck would have. I also found out the reason he had kept disappearing earlier in the reception: to sneak some apple pie moonshine, not to be with a woman. My irrational jealousy went away.

Did I mention how I'm shy, introverted, and socially awkward? I didn't feel that way with Joe, though. In fact, when the reception was over and it was time to leave, I took the initiative with a guy for the first time in my life.

"If I give you my number, will you use it?" I asked him. It was lame, but it was all I had.

"Yes," Joe replied. We exchanged numbers on cocktail napkins, and he walked me to my truck. As we stood there, I half expected him to kiss me, since it was clear we didn't want the night to end but had no good way to extend it. But what I got instead was just as sweet.

"You know, I feel a little inadequate walking you out to your truck when I just have my car here," he joked. "I like that you drive a truck, though. It's intriguing."

"Yeah, well, I only drove my truck because the wedding was in town," I said nervously. "I have a car for driving to school, but I live here, so . . ."

Joe laughed and hugged me.

The next day, while competing with Norman, I was talking with a friend. She was heading to a rodeo the next weekend in Klamath Falls, where Joe was going to school. She asked if I wanted to meet her there so we could hang out after she competed. I agreed because I wanted to support her, but mostly because it was an excuse to try to see Joe again.

Once I was back at school in Idaho, I called Joe. I knew if I followed all the "rules" of dating, I'd wait until he called me. But something wouldn't let me wait. I wasn't into playing the standard games under normal conditions, and I wasn't going to risk this on a game. So I called, pacing around my house and sweating profusely.

When Joe answered, I said, "Hey, it's Autumn from the wedding. . . . I'm going to the Klamath rodeo to watch a friend compete on Saturday. Would you be interested in coming and hanging out?"

After a short silence on Joe's end, his response wasn't what I had wanted. "I, um, will have to get back to you," he said. "I had a good time last weekend, I'm just not sure I can make it work."

I assumed this was the same as a no but with less risk of conflict. So I gave up on hearing from him again and sat around anxiously *not* waiting for the phone to ring and trying to figure out how I could get out of going to the rodeo with my friend. An eight-and-a-half-hour drive each way seemed a lot less fun without Joe being the prize at the end of it. But finally, Joe got back to me and agreed to meet me at the rodeo.

Once we had been together for a while, I learned the reason for Joe's hesitation that day. He had been raised to have morals and treat women properly, and he couldn't agree to going to the rodeo with me because he was dating another girl. So he had a choice to make: continue dating the girl who attended the same college as him, or take a risk on a girl who was almost nine hours away. Logically, he knew that dating me didn't make sense; no one looks for a long-distance relationship. Yet he had found himself thinking about me. After a few days, he called a friend to talk it over and see if he had any advice. While he was on the phone, his girlfriend walked into his dorm room. Apparently she had decided it was time that they break up. As soon as she left, he called me and we made plans.

I was so excited and anxious to see him. And since I wasn't much of a sharer, I didn't tell anyone that I was meeting him. He arrived late to the fairgrounds where the rodeo was being held, and I was so nervous that he wasn't going to show up, so I was relieved when he did. Much later, I found out he had locked his keys in the car right before he needed to leave. He didn't want to take the time to call a tow truck to unlock the doors, so he broke the smallest window in order to get to the rodeo and not keep me waiting.

After the rodeo, I got a message from my friend. She said she had to head back home and we'd have to catch up another night. It was late, and I didn't want to drive the two hours to my parents in Bend. So it was the perfect excuse to spend more time with Joe. I booked a hotel room, and we spent the night talking. We got maybe three hours of sleep, yet I wasn't all that tired as I drove back to school. Something in my life had just clicked into place.

3

Fʀᴏᴍ ᴛʜᴀᴛ ɴɪɢʜᴛ ꜰᴏʀᴡᴀʀᴅ, ᴊᴏᴇ and I talked every night. The only exception was during the summer, when he worked as a wildland firefighter. If he was assigned to a fire, he would usually camp nearby until the blaze was contained. Often he was outside cell phone coverage. On those nights, I'd just call and leave a message.

Sometimes our conversations would last for hours. Other times, they would last just long enough to say we were busy. But no matter what, we talked—so much that his mom, who paid for his cell phone, got a rather large bill, and we had to limit our talking time to nights and weekends so we didn't go over the allotted minutes. We talked about everything: our pasts, goals and dreams for the future, passions, and hopes. We talked about nothing important, but each word brought us closer together.

Over Memorial Day weekend, less than a month after we had met, we were hanging out in my parents' hot tub while they were out of town. It was only the second time we had seen each other, but since we'd both driven some distance to be together, it was clear that something was there. The night was clear, and the stars were shining down on us brightly.

"What are you looking for?" Joe asked, breaking the comfortable silence.

I realized I was scared. Scared of giving too much of myself, and scared of being hurt. I was typically a planner, but for once in my life I was enjoying following my heart and living in the moment, acting without thinking. Now Joe was asking me to use my head, look into the future, and I respected him too much not to be honest with him.

"I don't know," I said. "I haven't really thought about it. We spend most of our time over four hundred miles apart. I had just figured this would be a summer thing. How is more even possible?" I wanted to be around him, but I was so scared of being hurt. "I'm scared," I whispered, avoiding his gaze.

We sat there for a few minutes, listening to the frogs and the occasional car on the road. Eventually, Joe turned me so I was looking at him, lifting my face up so he could look in my eyes.

"I can't promise I won't hurt you, but I can promise I won't hurt you on purpose," he said. "I can't imagine going back to a life that you aren't in." His words were carefully thought out, words he knew to be true; and the truth was the only thing he could give me. And it was enough. We were together, and that was all that mattered.

THAT SUMMER WE SPENT as much time as possible together, which was limited by my job in Sunriver, Oregon, and his wild-land firefighting outside Burns. So it took two hours for us to drive to each other on the rare occasions we were both off from work. But it was enough for us. Just the thought of seeing each other made all the driving time worthwhile. More than once I'd drive to Burns to find out he had just been sent to a fire, so I'd sleep in his room. Sometimes he would come home before I had to return to Bend, and other times he wouldn't. It didn't matter, though. We were disappointed when we didn't see each other, but it was still worth the risk; we'd continue to plan and drive, living on the hope that we might get to spend a few hours together.

As summer neared its end, we talked about Joe moving up to Idaho to finish his degree, but in the end, we decided it didn't make sense. When school started in the fall, I returned to the University of Idaho and Joe to the Oregon Institute of Technology; we took turns driving the eight hours whenever we could just to see each other for a day and a half.

Joe treated me in a courteous, gentle manner I wasn't used to. In return, I responded in ways that were equally unfamiliar but just felt right. For example, as our relationship grew, Joe would stand patiently at the car door and wait for a kiss before I climbed in, no matter how much of a hurry he was in. Guys had tried to open my door in the past. When that had happened, I had usually rushed to get it myself. It had seemed like a patronizing act, and I was perfectly capable of getting my own door. But with Joe, it was different. It felt caring, not patronizing. It felt like respect.

While Joe was constantly taking care of me, he also encouraged my independence. He never questioned my ability to do something. Instead, he would stand by, ready to help when I needed it. I needed to feel capable, and I loved how proud he was of me when I did things on my own, no matter if I was taking apart my car door panel and correctly putting it back together or jerry-rigging his cordless drill so it would work as a mixer when I made him brownies. Joe would always smile at me with pride in his eyes and brag about me to his friends. Just his presence was encouraging to me; I could do anything with him by my side.

Joe and I were drawn to each other. We didn't need to be with each other all the time. But when we were together, we wanted to be as close as possible. I'd sit next to him in the middle of his truck's bench seat as he drove us around. It was more important to be close to Joe than to enjoy the comfort of the passenger seat by the window.

We spent that Christmas with my family. Joe had already met my parents, but at Christmas he was introduced to the rest of my family, including my cousin Brittany. While Joe quickly and easily charmed my family, he was most drawn to Brittany. I'm not sure if this was because she was my favorite relative or because he appreciated that she was quiet and soft-spoken.

Joe's family was small, and his family gatherings often ended with everyone reading quietly or watching a football game. My family, on the other hand, is all conversation, usually held in "outside" voices. While Joe held his own as manners dictated, I noticed that his stress levels increased while we were there, along with his use of Copenhagen tobacco.

Brittany, Joe, and I would eventually drift to the barn or the den, where we could talk quietly or sit in silence. I was happy to see Joe and Brittany get along and carry on easy conversation on their own. I was even happier when Brittany told me simply that she was happy for me and Joe was a keeper.

After that first Christmas, Joe would try to find an escape from the noise and craziness at all my family events. The second Christmas we spent with my family, for example, I spent Christmas Eve morning making apple, lemon meringue, and other pies that had been requested. Joe, however, was left to fend for himself. When I was done, I found him in the den with Brittany, my sister's husband, and my maternal grandfather, who we called Grandpa Chuck. They were happily hanging out together in silence, without feeling any pressure to socialize. I smiled when I recognized it wasn't an awkward silence, but a relaxed one.

Joe and I continued our long-distance relationship for two and a half years, racking up huge gas bills and putting thousands of miles on our cars. During the summers our long-distance relationship wasn't quite as long, and we made every effort to spend time together. I'd stay with him in Burns during my days off, then drive two hours back to Bend for work and summer school. This increased my chances of seeing him when he wasn't working on a fire. Neither of us kept track of who drove the most miles or sacrificed the most. All that mattered was seeing each other as much as possible. On weekends when it didn't work out because of classes, jobs at college, or other reasons, we'd be disappointed. But such was life, and we'd make up for it by spending hours on the phone.

During one such weekend, I was sitting in my living room in Idaho, partially listening to the TV while studying, when Joe called. "Hey, I just saw on TV that you might be able to see the northern lights from Idaho tonight," he said. "You should go outside and check."

I didn't think anything of it, but when I went outside, the northern lights weren't awaiting me. Instead, Joe was standing there on the porch. It was a complete surprise; and since I wasn't used to being romantic, I couldn't have imagined anything better than that. It even beat the time he made me breakfast in bed on a tray, decorated with flowers he had pilfered from a house down the street.

While we were devoted to each other, we were still in college, and we understood and accepted that we had lives outside of our relationship. We would both go out on occasion, usually on the weekends when we couldn't see each other. But on occasion, Joe, who was more social than I was, would hang out with his friends in the evening, especially when he was waiting for me to drive down to Klamath Falls.

One weekend, he took it a little too far. I had skipped out of my last class that day and left early, so I arrived at Klamath Falls around dark. As was our standard, I called him when I reached Klamath Lake, far enough out of town that he could get home to meet me. However, this time he admitted he was a little inebriated and probably shouldn't drive, so he would send his roommate home and have him pick me up and bring me to the party. I wasn't in the best humor after the long drive, and finding out that Joe was unable to drive—and apparently unwilling to ride along with his roommate—rubbed me the wrong way.

By the time I arrived at the party with Joe's roommate, I was in no mood to be social. So I asked his roommate to send Joe out, then waited by Joe's truck. When Joe came out a few minutes later, it was clear he wasn't in a rational state of mind. His baseball hat was cocked to one side of his head, which was typical as he became more drunk. He came to give me a kiss and a hug, and somehow he grasped the fact that I was upset. So he continued to hold me; and with each passing minute, the weight he was putting on me increased as he used all of my five-foot, eight-inch frame to support his six feet and three inches. He apologized profusely for not meeting me and for being a little intoxicated, and promised over and over that he would make it up to me with strawberry waffles in the morning.

Realizing Joe was fading fast, I loaded him into his truck and told his friends we were heading home. They informed me that he had found the Pendleton whiskey a little too smooth when mixed with Coke and consumed most of a fifth of it. I climbed into the driver's seat of Joe's old Chevy truck, which was painted blue with his custom flames decorating the rocker panels in white, and made it clear to Joe that this was not what I had driven so far for. Then I raced the truck through two stop signs, braking and accelerating as quickly as I could before I had to stop so he could throw up. After that, I took him home, feeling pity for him. I got him into bed and tried to force him to take water and ibuprofen, only to have him pass out and continue to hurl all over the bed.

There wasn't much I could do, especially since Joe was six inches taller than me and at least sixty pounds heavier. So I rolled him around on the bed, laying down towels and trying to keep him on his side so he wouldn't choke while I looked up the symptoms of alcohol poisoning and tried to decide whether to call an ambulance. Looking back, I should have dialed 911. But as a broke college kid, I hesitated and spent a sleepless night on the floor instead. Around dawn, I was satisfied that Joe was OK and went into the living room to watch TV. If I hadn't been so tired, I probably would have hit him when he came sauntering into the living room all chipper and rested, as if nothing had happened. In fact, I had to remind him of what happened the night before, only convincing him when he went back into the bedroom to look under the towels he had slept on.

He kept his word, though. I got strawberry waffles for breakfast that morning—and a good story to hold over his head.

WE MADE SURE WE were together as often as possible. It was especially important that we used that time to do things we both loved. One of those things was branding at the ranch every spring.

Joe had wanted nothing more than to work with cows and live on a ranch. Brandings were as close as Joe could get to living the life of a traditional cowboy, and he reveled in it. Branding would occur every April, when most of the calves had been born but before they were sent out on the range to graze for the summer. Typically the brandings were held in a large corral located at the base of a hill, situated between the long driveway to the ranch house, an alfalfa field, and the calving ground.

Brandings were always a big event in and around Burns. Friends and family from all over the county would come and help their neighbors brand, vaccinate, and castrate calves. The brandings would start first thing in the morning and go into the afternoon, depending on the number of calves. Once the last calf was branded, and the animals turned back out into the pasture, everyone would load up their horses and drive to the ranch house, where Joe's grandpa would host a big meal as thanks for their help. This was typically when everyone would sit around, catch up with each other, and talk about the day's work.

The first time I went to a branding with Joe, I hung out with the ground crew, helping where I could and taking pictures. Joe was a good roper. His goal was to be as good as his grandpa, and I always wanted to catch the loops Joe would be proud of in photographs, though I was happy just to snap pictures of him sitting strong and confident on his horse.

We both spent that first branding together working, each doing our separate jobs with the warm spring sun shining down on us, cows stirring up dust, and horses twirling around us. The smell of livestock and burning hair filled my nose, while the sounds of flying ropes, occasional four-letter words, and bawling calves filled my ears.

To minimize the calves' stress and make the process as easy on them as possible, we would pull them to the fire by their back legs. I'd watch the cows, hovering nearby to ensure their protective instincts didn't cause them to charge at the other workers. To many people, a scene like this—a small corral teeming with cows, calves, horseback riders with ropes, and workers on the ground running to and from the branding fire—would seem like chaos. But in reality, it was an organized process that had been passed down for generations. Joe and I knew why branding was necessary, but thanks to one conversation we had after that first branding, I also knew that a part of Joe was sorry about it.

"I love branding, but sometimes I feel just a touch sad when it's over," Joe said, looking out over the freshly branded calves that were now resting peacefully.

"Why?" I asked, trying to read the expression on his face.

"Well, I guess it's because before branding, the calves are so carefree. They run around, jump, and play. Nothing has marked them yet. After branding, they still act like that some, but not as much. It's like branding them breaks their spirit a little. It forces them to grow up. It marks the line between frolicking calf and beef cow. I don't know. Maybe it's just because they're getting older, just a coincidence."

We sat there in silence as the sun slowly set, leaving a splash of color in the clear sky.

WHILE JOE AND I cherished our summers together, Joe's responsibilities as a wildland firefighter during the season meant he spent many nights—sometimes up to three weeks—away from home. We did OK when we had to be apart. After all, you have to be OK with time apart when you're in a long-distance relationship. Still, I always had such an urgency to be with him as much as possible. For example, one weekend when Joe was firefighting, I traveled seven hours away to a music festival with a friend. I hadn't heard from Joe in days when he finally called Saturday evening. He told me he was on his way home. He thought he would be able to spend the night in Burns, but he would likely head out to another wildfire in the morning.

That was all I needed: just a little hope that I'd get to see him. I didn't make my friend leave the concert, but I did convince her that we needed to head home as soon as it was over so I could see Joe. We left a little after midnight, narrowly missed a moose, and drove through the night. About forty-five minutes from home, I got another call from Joe. He said work had called him in and he had to leave. I missed seeing him by less than an hour and had to wait another week before he came home again.

Once I graduated from the University of Idaho in the fall of 2006, I moved to Klamath Falls and lived with Joe while he finished his degree. For the first time since our relationship began in May 2004, we could finally spend more than a few weeks together. And as we happily found out, living together was even better.

We matured together. When we had met, I was twenty and Joe was nineteen, and we were young, confused, and trying to find our way in life. Now, we knew what we wanted from life. We would talk and dream with each other. When Joe would take me to the ranch, we'd ride horseback together and share our dreams about the future.

"What do you want to do after college?" I asked him once, noticing how the sun glinted off the silver on his saddle.

"Come back here," he said as he looked over the land he loved. "Help Dad and Grandpa with the ranch. I'll probably have to work, though. Either keep working as a firefighter, or maybe I can get a job as an engineer. What about you?"

I shrugged and gave him a quick smile. "I have no idea. Get a job. Hang out with you."

By the time we moved in together, our conversations had changed from individual dreams to our dreams. "What's the plan for when you're done with school?" I asked as we went for a drive one day, my head on his shoulder and his hand holding mine tightly.

"We'll go back to Burns," Joe said as he squeezed my hand. "Buy a house. You can get a job in town, and I'll get one until we can buy enough cows to make up part of the income. We'll get married and have some kids and be together, and that's all that matters. That we're together."

He was right. Being together was all that mattered. And because we wanted to be together, we molded ourselves into the best fit for the other while holding on to who we were. We each had our flaws, but we learned about them together and adapted as we grew. Most people think you finish growing in high school. But for us, we grew so much as young adults during college and those few years afterward.

While we had known for a long time that we'd eventually get married, Joe hadn't wanted to make it official until he had finished school. It was important to him to know he could take care of a wife and a family, to make sure we had a home and he a job. That way, I wouldn't need to work, so I could stay home with our future kids if I wanted to. He wanted to be sure he could give us everything we wanted. It wasn't because I needed to be taken care of. Rather, it was a sign of his respect for me that he wanted to be able to be a man and provide for his family.

So when Joe proposed on Valentine's Day in 2009, he completely surprised me. I had been out of town for two weeks for training with one of my coworkers. She told me she thought Joe would propose. I shot her down, believing he wouldn't be so predictable.

I had known Joe would propose at some point. We had already wandered around jewelry stores, looking at rings and talking about how the "rule" of spending three months' pay on an engagement ring was ridiculous. He knew I liked sapphires more than diamonds and preferred white gold over gold. He also knew I'd say yes, but apparently that doesn't take the anxiety out of proposing.

Maybe I was convinced that Joe would do something more unique. He had talked about wanting to make it special, but the challenge he faced was that I'd already be expecting the proposal. Maybe he figured the best way to surprise me was to take an approach that was more traditional, on a day made for couples. Sometimes it felt like Joe knew me better than I knew myself.

When I got home on Valentine's Day, Joe told me I needed to pack a bag. We were heading to another town for the night; he had gotten us a hotel room, dinner reservations, and tickets to a show. We didn't usually celebrate Valentine's Day, since we didn't need to. We had love every day. But he said he had missed me, and so he decided to do something special.

Something seemed off when we first walked into the hotel room. Joe had been so excited, and suddenly he seemed a little down.

"What's wrong?" I asked.

"I expected the room to be nicer," he said. "I remember as a kid that these hotels were always the fanciest. I guess things have changed over the last twenty years."

His concern didn't make sense to me. The hotel room wasn't much different from others we had stayed in before. I didn't think about it too much, though, as I got ready for dinner while he lounged on the bed and watched TV. When it was time to go, Joe went to open the door for me. But instead of opening it, he turned around.

"Will you marry me?" he asked as he stood there, holding a ring.

"What? Really?" I said. For a few seconds, I was confused about what was happening. But as I looked at Joe, a smile slowly spread across my face. A rush of warmth flushed over me.

To prove he was serious, Joe got down on one knee and asked

again. "Marry me. Be my wife." His brown eyes were full of antic-
ipation and hope.

"Yes! Always and forever, yes." I saw the happiness that bright-
ened Joe's face, and I knew the look on my face matched it. He
stood up, slowly slid the ring on my finger, and gave me a gentle
kiss to seal the deal.

Joe may have been disappointed in the room, but I thought
it was perfect. And after the proposal, it didn't seem to matter to
him either. Throughout the night, we couldn't keep the smiles off
our faces; I wore my ring proudly, like it had always belonged on
my hand.

"No regrets?" Joe would ask on occasion.

"No regrets," I'd answer.

Now that we were officially engaged, we started planning our
future. Less then two months later, over spring break, we made
an offer on a house. Joe graduated in June and spent most of the
summer at a guard station fighting fire an hour south of Burns.
Then in September, we married. The ceremony occurred at the
place Joe loved more than anywhere else: his family's ranch, on the
lawn under the giant trees planted generations earlier. We honey-
mooned in Yellowstone and Glacier National Parks, and also spent
a few days at his uncle's cabin in Montana.

Life was perfect. We were surrounded by friends and family.
In October 2010, a work party composed of both of our families
helped us build a porch on our house. A month later, we went
to Eugene and helped my aunt, uncle, and cousin Brittany finish
her new training barn and arena. While Brittany was quiet and
soft-spoken, she knew exactly what she wanted when it came
to her horses. She set us out on tasks that were aligned with
our skills. In particular, she kept Joe for herself. All weekend
long, she would ask for his opinion about different elements

of construction and engineering, and he would use his skills to reach her level of perfection.

"How does this look?" Joe asked at one point. "Is that how you want it?"

"Move it a little to the left," Brittany answered. "Do you want the level?"

"Yes. And hand me the drill, please."

"Sure thing."

Joe was perfectly happy working with Brittany. He didn't have to carry on small talk, and she listened to his advice. They each had their role and were able to carry it out without a lot of discussion. One of my favorite pictures from that day shows them standing back and admiring—and, in all likelihood, judging—the work they had just completed, content in their companionship, Joe holding his coffee cup as usual.

Joe and I spent a few years enjoying our marriage. We traveled, hung out with friends, and went to concerts. We learned to play tennis (where Joe hogged the ball, since he didn't trust me to actually hit it when it came onto my side of the court) and went snowboarding (where the skills Joe learned in one day exceeded all the skills I had developed in ten years). We celebrated holidays and birthdays and participated in a stick horse rodeo, which I was lucky enough to get on video. I lectured him on wearing his seat belt and convinced him to give up his Copenhagen. Everything we did, we did it together, and that was what mattered. We judged other couples who complained about their spouses or argued a lot, and talked about how lucky we were that our life was so amazing. In 2011, we decided we were ready to have kids, so we determined when having a baby would best fit our schedule. (Yes, I like to plan and have that much control over my life.)

And guess what? I got pregnant right on schedule. Life was easy, and everything was perfect—so much so that sometimes, maybe out of a lack of trust in the universe, we'd talk about when our good luck would run out.

4

ODY WAS BORN ON FEBRUARY 17, 2012. The labor went quickly and relatively easily, with no real complications. I opted not to use an epidural or pain medications, since I liked to control what I could in my life. Everything went to plan. Joe took to fatherhood instantly, learning to swaddle and change diapers like a pro while I struggled to keep up with him. He loved being a dad and having a family. His number-one goal in life was to provide me and Cody not only with the necessities, but also with love and time. He wanted to include us no matter the endeavor. He wanted to teach Cody to be respectful and have good manners, hunt and fish, ride and rope, throw a baseball and fix a car. In short, he wanted to give us the best life possible.

Being a planner (a term I prefer over *control freak*), I wanted our kids to be about two years apart. So in 2013, when it was time to try again, we were happy to get pregnant right away. Feeling excited and blessed, we went in for an early ultrasound to determine a more accurate due date.

The baby was measuring right around six weeks, which matched our expectations. But no heartbeat was detected. The doctor told us I had likely experienced a miscarriage and my body hadn't realized it yet. However, there was a chance the baby was still developing, and its heart just hadn't started. So we went home and waited to see what happened.

Something about waiting zaps all the energy out of you. I

tried to be hopeful, but there wasn't much to hope for. So I'd pace around the house restlessly, walking from the kitchen to the living room just to feel like I was doing something. On occasion I'd stop and stare out the window to watch the world still moving, oblivious to my hurt. I'd go to work to occupy myself, but I only went through the motions. My mind was too numb and my heart too pained to be productive. So we waited each day for my body to miscarry the fetus, yet I hoped and prayed for our baby to survive.

Because that's what was supposed to happen—or so I had thought. After all, life had been perfect and easy up to that point. We were good people, and we didn't deserve loss or sadness. I had planned this second pregnancy, and a miscarriage wasn't part of that. Our kids needed to be close in age so they could play and go to school together. They needed to experience life together, to be best friends like Joe and his brother were. This was what we had planned. This was how our life was supposed to go. Everything Joe and I had planned for our future was contingent on having this baby. Without it, the age gap would be too big, and I worried our kids wouldn't have a close sibling relationship. That was what I was really worried about. I was afraid that, without that relationship, the rest of my plans would fall apart—that I really wasn't in control of my future.

When we went back to the hospital a week later, we hoped to detect a heartbeat. But I tried to keep my expectations low. I didn't want to be disappointed again, and the doctor was pretty sure we'd already lost the baby. This time, I knew the quiet ultrasound technician meant bad news. No measurements were discussed. No signs of the baby's development were shown. There was only silence and the sound of our hearts slowly breaking, shattering on the floor around us like broken glass.

I laid on the table, looking at our baby and holding Joe's hand as tears ran down my cheeks. How could I fail so much? How could I let my husband down?

We couldn't wait for my body to handle the miscarriage on its own. The risk of infection was increasing, and my body still wasn't showing signs of giving up the baby. The doctor gave me two options: have surgery to remove the baby and associated tissues, or take a prescribed medication that would cause my body to discard it naturally. I chose the latter, then took the medication at home and waited for my body to respond.

I stayed up late, wrapped in a blanket in the living room recliner. Joe made sure I was as comfortable as possible, then went to bed. I may have told him he could go. He had to work the next day, and I didn't want him to see me cry. I still felt as though I had failed Joe in some way. Providing Joe with children was part of my job as a woman and as his wife. No one else could give him that, and I had failed. I didn't want my failure, and my resulting sadness, to affect him more than it had to. So we grieved alone, not talking about our loss or showing the pain we felt.

My body completed the miscarriage that night. I was alone in the living room while Joe was alone in our bedroom. I didn't recognize that I was grieving. I didn't even know what grief was then. I recognize it now, but I'm a different person today than I was in 2013.

I'd eat out of reflex, but food tasted like cardboard in my mouth. I was so distracted and tired. I wanted to sleep, but at night I'd lie there, thinking about our loss. It seemed strange to love something so much when it was hardly more than an idea, to miss something—or, rather, someone—I had barely known. But I missed the baby, down to my core. I didn't know what to do with my sadness over never seeing its face looking up at me in wonder, the loss of all the should-have-beens.

I also grieved the plans we had made, the future I had imagined, where Cody would play with a brother or sister two years younger than him. I walked around for a few days in that comforting fog that follows loss, the fog that protects you from feeling more than you can handle. I grieved my loss of control and the loss of my innocence. Now I knew the awful parts of life could happen to us. Just because we were good people didn't mean we would be protected from the bad. And in place of my innocence, fear began to grow. Fear of what could happen despite my plans, despite my hope, despite my best efforts to create the life I wanted.

Joe stayed with me for a few days, taking care of me and trying to distract me. Maybe he was trying to distract himself too. I knew he was grieving, even though he tried to hide it from me. The day Joe went back to work, I stood at the big living room window that overlooked the valley below, trying not to think or feel. Joe came up behind me, wrapped his arms around me, and pulled me toward him. "Do I need to worry about you?" he whispered in my ear. His voice strained with the effort it took him to ask that question. "Will you be OK alone?"

"Yes," I whispered back. I knew Joe was asking if I'd hurt myself, and I didn't lie. I knew I'd be physically OK; I just didn't know if I'd ever be emotionally OK again.

I knew Joe felt the loss too. I could see the sadness in his face when he didn't think I was looking, and I'd catch him staring blankly out the window. But his grief was different from mine. To him, the baby was an abstract concept. He grieved the loss of his future with the baby, and I could tell from his expression that he was hurting for me. But a part of me and my body still ached from losing the baby; and with my loss, the feeling of failure settled even deeper. I probably knew then that I hadn't truly failed Joe, but what you know and what you feel aren't always in line.

I didn't want to hurt myself. But as I stood by that window, watching my husband leave for work, I thought it wouldn't be difficult to imagine an outlet for all the pain in my heart. I could see how physical pain could become that outlet. Physical pain was so much easier to manage than emotional pain. This was the turning point for me. As I stood at that window, looking at the blue sky and wondering how people could survive such losses, I knew somewhere deep down that love and hope was how they survived, and I could feel that love and hope in the arms wrapped around me.

In hindsight, I didn't give Joe enough credit for recognizing my grief and depression. It takes strength to consider that someone you love may contemplate self-harm or suicide. It takes even more strength to talk to that person about it. Knowing Joe really saw me and the pain I was in made all the difference in the world. He didn't chastise me for crying. He didn't tell me I needed to be strong. He didn't tell me it was part of God's plan, or that it happened for a reason. Instead, he let me be sad. He let me know he was there and always would be. With Joe's support, I was able to accept the loss. I was able to remind myself that I hadn't failed anyone—not myself, not Joe, and not our beautiful baby who was somewhere in heaven, wrapped in the arms of an angel.

While I didn't feel OK at that moment, I knew I'd eventually be OK as long as I had Joe with me. We could survive anything if we were together. So in my grief, I learned how to live with the loss. I also held on to the hope that the doctor was right when she said miscarriages are unfortunate but common. Since we'd had a healthy baby already, there was no reason to think we couldn't have another. With Joe by my side, I picked up my shattered heart and began to piece it back together. As soon as I was cleared by the doctor, we tried to get pregnant again, and I thanked God that the proverbial shoe had dropped. Our lives were a little less easy and a little less perfect. But we could breathe and get back to planning our lives and our future.

A few months later, we were expecting again. We were elated that the kids would still be near that magical two-year range. But we were also cautious. Gone were the days when we'd look forward to each appointment, carefree and full of hopes and dreams. Now, each appointment was tinged with apprehension. After all, our lives were mostly easy and perfect. A miscarriage couldn't happen again, not to us.

We went in for an early ultrasound once again. I walked in with a tightness in my chest and a fear that hadn't been present before. I started crying at the quiet in the room; to me, too much quiet signaled that something was wrong. The ultrasound technician worked in silence, measuring and taking notes. And in that silence, I felt my fragile heart break again. If that breaking had been a sound, it would have been deafening.

I held Joe's hand as the technician delivered the news: we were pregnant with twins, and they were measuring about nine weeks, but there were no heartbeats. There was no waiting period this time. We were given the same options as the first time, though we were told that the medication might not be successful due to the size of the babies. We chose to try it anyway. That way, I could avoid an unnecessary surgery that could cause scar tissue to develop.

We went home, holding hands in silence. There weren't any words left to say. We didn't have dinner that night; neither of us felt like eating. I took the medication, and Joe tucked a blanket around me, making sure I was comfortable before he went to bed. I settled into the chair and waited. The TV was on, but I didn't watch it. It was a poor attempt to distract myself from thinking about or feeling our newest loss. Eventually the darkness and sadness surrounded me as my body repelled our babies and silent tears rolled down my cheeks.

I felt grief and loss once again. But more than that, I felt defeated. One of my main responsiblities as a wife, as a woman, was to provide my husband and myself with children. But out of three pregnancies and four babies, so far I had delivered only one healthy baby. And while I loved Cody with everything I had, I still felt like I had failed Joe as well as myself.

This time, I knew I was grieving. That knowledge helped in some ways. Not only did I know what to expect, but I also knew how much it would hurt. I would cry and scream, but I had survived it before. And I knew I could survive again.

In an attempt to make ourselves feel better and give ourselves hope for the future, Joe and I agreed that this was the second proverbial shoe dropping. We hadn't expected the first miscarriage. Neither had we expected this one, but the possibility of it happening had been there. Now that our pair of proverbial shoes had dropped, we didn't have to hold our breath anymore. We could move forward with our life together and accept it was even less easy and even less perfect. Now that we had our share of loss, what else could go wrong?

For the first time, I recognized on some level that misery truly does love company. Before our miscarriages, I hadn't known anyone who'd had one—or so I had thought. According to the American College of Obstetricians and Gynecologists, around 10 percent of recognized pregnancies end in a miscarriage. Women just don't talk about them. When I returned to the land management agency where Joe and I both worked, four of my female coworkers asked why I had been gone. Joe had told them I didn't feel well. I, however, decided to tell them about the miscarriage. As I stood there in the reception area, surrounded by those women, I was surprised when all of them said they either had a miscarriage or knew someone who had.

None of them shared their stories. However, personally knowing other women who had felt the same loss and defeat gave me a bit of comfort. No one else had had my exact experience, but they still knew. Just hearing an acknowledgment of miscarriages made me feel less alone.

But I was still sad. I was in a light fog and felt confused and guilty. But after a few weeks, I started to pretend I was OK. That I didn't lie awake, long after Joe had fallen asleep, to cry.

I felt the world expected me to be OK. To just move on, get over it, and go back to being the person I had been before. After all, miscarriages happen to lots of people. So I did. On the outside, I did what was expected of me. But on the inside, I fell into the darkness alone because I was unwilling to drag Joe with me. What I didn't understand, though, was that Joe had a darkness of his own. Even though this loss was more abstract to him, I wasn't protecting him from it by not talking about it. Instead, it isolated us from each other in our grief. I sacrificed the comfort my husband would have gladly provided by putting on a brave face and pretending everything was the same. Inside, though, I was groping around in the darkness, worried that I wouldn't be able to escape.

A FEW WEEKS AFTER I had returned to work, we headed down to Las Vegas for the National Finals Rodeo with a couple of friends. Joe, being an engineer, was excited to tour the Hoover Dam. As we walked through the dam's tunnels, he looked in awe at the massive concrete structure, which, according to the Bureau of Reclamation, provides electricity for about 1.3 million people in

Nevada, Arizona, and California. He was clearly fascinated by its construction and the huge turbine generators.

Before the tour, however, we stood on top of the dam, Joe holding his cowboy hat in place to keep from the wind from stealing it. "I can't believe we're going on the dam tour," he said. "Do you think our guide's name will be Arnie? I wonder if we'll be able to ask dam questions." His eyes twinkled with excitement as he threw his head back and laughed at his own joke.

At the Mob Museum, Joe took his turn standing for a mug shot while I pretended to be the cop who put him there. Then we went to the rodeo, spending too much money on beer and greasy food while watching the best cowboys in the world compete. We talked about how awesome it was that his grandpa was at this level in the 1960s.

At the rodeo afterparty, which was packed with hundreds of people, Joe got drunk enough that he wanted to do the cha cha slide. "I can do that," he said, watching as the dance began. "Hold my drink." I did, and he made his way to the edge of the dance floor.

What I witnessed next made me laugh so hard that I almost cried. Joe would clap his hands when he was supposed to slide, and then slide when he was supposed to stomp. His cha-cha could only be described as an unrhythmic wiggling, with his arms and legs waving in all directions.

"Nailed it," Joe said as he walked off the dance floor, hat tilted to the side and a big smile on his face. "What are you laughing at?" he asked me, oblivious to the hilarious show he had just given. Without waiting for my answer, he declared, "I want cake!" and went off in search of it.

We made memories during that trip. Despite our grief, we laughed, loved, and lived. And with Joe by my side, I remembered that life wasn't all darkness. Even with sadness dominating my world, there were still flickers of light, happiness, and laughter. I just had to be willing to latch on to those moments.

The trip pulled me out of my acute grief, but a few days after we got home, I woke up with a migraine. This was nothing new; I had gotten this kind of headache before. However, about thirty minutes after Joe left for work, the pain became excruciating. Medication wasn't working, and I couldn't do anything but cry. I called Joe and told him I needed him. He asked no questions; he just came home, looked at me, and brought me into the emergency room. I was nauseous, could barely talk, and thought my head was going to explode. But even though I was in so much pain, the doctors refused to give me something for it. Instead, they added to my frustration by asking about my medical history, including the miscarriages.

Eventually they gave me morphine. I felt warm and fuzzy afterward, and the pain in my head eased into a gentle pulse. Once I calmed down enough to talk, the doctors explained what was happening.

While I had thought I was over the most recent miscarriage, it wasn't done with me. Some parts of the placenta or babies had remained in my body. As a result, I had developed a severe uterine infection that required emergency surgery, along with large doses of antibiotics.

I don't remember much about that day, given that I was high on morphine. But I do remember that Joe was by my side the entire time. The on-call doctor came in dressed in camouflage because he had been out hunting. I found it funny and apologized that I was ruining his day off. The thought of bothering others or causing them to worry horrified me. Even in my morphine-induced state,

I preferred to be on the periphery, someone who was present but not noticed.

After the surgery was over, I woke up to find Joe sitting next to me. I had seen him worried about me in the past. But I had never seen him look as scared as he did at that moment, violently shaking and shivering as I regained consciousness. He thought I was having a seizure, that he was losing me. I had never doubted that Joe loved me. But in that moment, I knew he really did, and that was all that mattered.

5

I TOOK A FEW WEEKS off from work to recover from my infection and the surgery. Between the physical discomfort and the knowledge of the incomplete miscarriage, my insomnia returned. I would sleep for no more than four hours each night. My feelings of guilt and failure returned, along with anger. I felt life was dragging me down again after I had finally started to heal from our loss. I didn't want to eat, and I did what I could to prevent my depression from affecting others, especially Cody and Joe. I also tried to convince myself that both of the proverbial shoes had dropped. One . . . two . . . so that was it, right? No more waiting anxiously for what would come next, right? That was what I kept telling myself, but my heart didn't believe it. My mind kept going back to the saying "Trouble comes in threes," and that made me sad and fearful.

I wanted to have another child with Joe, but I was scared that it wouldn't happen. Fear gripped my life in ways I had never experienced. I was scared that I'd continue to let Joe and myself down. These miscarriages had opened my eyes to a world where terrible things happened, even to good people. I would find myself thinking about worst-case scenarios, like injury or disease. I feared that something bad would happen to me, Cody, or Joe.

This way of thinking was a vicious cycle. I would become more depressed, which would make me feel awful for not being the wife and mom I should be, which would make me even more depressed.

This was the first time I recognized I was truly depressed—or maybe I was just sad and grieving. When grief is involved, there isn't much of a difference between that and depression. I thought I wasn't the type of person who would be depressed. So I told myself it must just be sadness, which is totally normal, and my lack of sleep was making it worse.

So I got a prescription from the doctor for sleeping pills. They helped me sleep, but they didn't heal me. I had thought they would help fix what was wrong so I could go back to being me. But even with this most recent loss, I was too new to the experience to know there was no returning to the person I was before and I'd carry it forever. I was learning, though. I wasn't able to put it into words at the time, but I was realizing I could carry grief, and how I carried that grief was up to me. That was one thing that was in my control.

A FEW MONTHS LATER, Joe and I were expecting again. We went through the pregnancy in fear; I was constantly preparing myself for the loss. The relief I felt at the end of the early ultrasound, which detected the baby's strong heartbeat, was immense. Yet tension would build between appointments.

I knew I was being paranoid. I had no reason to worry, since everything was going smoothly. We passed the first trimester, but I had experienced too much loss to feel calm. As much as I wanted to control my life, I knew now that some things were beyond my control. I had been tossed into the real world, where shitty things happen to everyone. Even though I tried to keep my fear at bay, it often overwhelmed me, shadowing everything.

In the meantime, Joe lived in a way that seemed fearless to me. He took amazing care of Cody, loving, tickling, and playing with him. He built a huge playset in our backyard that was made of juniper trees and spare pieces of wood. Looking at it almost gave me splinters; and the slide was so steep, with a bump in the middle, that it sometimes launched Cody into the air. It was perfect.

Joe also put toys in his workshop and set up a baby swing. That way, he could watch Cody and the future baby when he was out there, if I needed him to. His excitement and ability to continue living life the best he could eventually brought me around, though I struggled. I was scared to believe it would all be OK. Even though we were well into the pregnancy and had had no issues, I was scared to hope it would work out this time. But Joe's love was greater than our loss and my fear. With his encouragement, we began to plan and look forward to our future with our perfect little family. He reminded me that living in hope was better than living in fear.

In the end, I experienced no complications with the pregnancy. Our second son, Wade, was born on January 23, 2015, after a quick and easy labor. He was the perfect completion to our little family, especially since we had decided two kids was enough. Though, to be honest, the decision had been mostly mine. I didn't want to risk more miscarriages, and I wasn't sure I had the energy to raise more than two kids. Cody alone was exhausting. Even though he was almost three, I still struggled to balance work and chores. I wasn't comfortable taking him to the store and keeping him happy while I was shopping. So I had no idea how I would manage both him and a baby.

As I lay in the hospital bed, holding Wade and watching Joe stroke his tiny hand, Joe looked at me and said, "It's too bad we have to cull you."

"What are you talking about?" I asked, tearing my gaze away from the beautiful baby in my arms.

"You make a pretty good cow," he replied, smiling. "You've produced two amazing boys for us and made it look so easy. . . . Well, at least compared to the stories you hear about having babies."

I couldn't help but laugh. What Joe had said was a very big compliment, worded in the ranching lingo he was so comfortable with.

While Joe supported my decision to not have any more kids, he loved his new son and probably would have jumped at the chance to have more. So he took precautions in case I changed my mind. His one rule was no permanent sterilization for five years. Looking back, I think he planned to wear me down and convince me that we should have more, though he never pressured me in any way. He must have known that eventually I'd want one more, and he wanted to make sure I still had the option. I didn't know then, but what a blessing that five-year rule was when he gave it to me.

WE BROUGHT WADE HOME and were over the moon. Joe was an amazing, hands-on father with Wade, just like he was for Cody. He took care of the baby and played with our oldest son so I could have time to heal and recover. "It isn't fair," he would say to me. "Just because you have the boobs and the milk doesn't mean you should get to hold Wade all the time." He would gladly take the baby whenever I wasn't feeding him, and he clearly wasn't thrilled about sharing Wade with our moms when they took turns staying with us. He would stay up at night with Wade, rocking him, talking to him, and just staring at the perfect little man we had made before bringing him to me for nursing.

One day, Joe was sitting on the couch, telling Wade the ins and outs of life. I stood up and walked over to them with my hands out, gesturing to take the baby even though it wasn't time to feed him. Joe pulled Wade toward his chest, wrapped his arms around the baby and himself, and glared at me with a ferocity I had rarely seen from him. "No!" he said. "This is my baby! You can't have him." It was one of the few times Joe told me no, and I had no chance of getting Wade from him at that point. Instead, I took a picture and let them continue to solve the world's problems. After all, Joe was going back to work soon, and I'd get to stay home and hold Wade all I wanted.

Another time, about a week or so after Wade was born, I was more tired than usual. So Joe swooped in and took over taking care of the kids. He sent me to bed, following me in to make sure I listened to him. Then he wrapped his arms around me, enveloping me in love and security. He told me how proud he was of me and our family, how happy he was, how he never knew such happiness existed, and how he couldn't ask for anything more. And then he apologized, saying he had no idea why he had been extra sappy and emotional since Wade had been born.

I pressed my head against his chest, listening to his heartbeat. "What would I do without you?" I asked. In that moment, I didn't know how I could live without him. He was everything to me, and he took care of me. I had said this before, when he really picked up my slack; he would reply, "I don't know, waste away?" or another joking response.

This time, he didn't reply in that flippant manner. Instead, he put his hands on my shoulders, gently pushed me back so he could look me in the eye, and brushed some stray, messy hairs away from my face. "You would be fine," he said. "Some amazing guy would show up at the front door to take care of you and the boys. He would love you and the boys like I love you." He was serious as he said this, and I could tell he believed every word. It was important to him that I knew this.

I rolled my eyes, doubting that I would be OK and that someone else would be willing to love me. Then I smiled. "Thank you
for being so amazing. I love you."

A FEW DAYS LATER, Joe was dead.

6

THE NEXT FEW WEEKS AFTER Joe's death were like a storm in the night. I was still recovering from the birth of Wade, so dealing with that as well as losing my husband made me feel like I was whirling around, confused and disoriented in the dark. But other people did their best to anchor me. By seven o'clock the morning after Joe died, a neighbor had already brought breakfast to the house to feed the growing number of people there. Support poured in from our rural community. The garbage company dropped off an extra can, and the local furniture store delivered an extra refrigerator. Friends and strangers alike brought food, household supplies, and gifts for me and the boys.

One of the men who stopped by was Kyle, a coworker of mine and Joe's who I didn't know very well. He came with paper towels, paper plates, garbage bags, and other practical items, as well as a toy tractor for Cody. Before he left, he asked my mom what he could do to help. She told him he could unload a trailer full of construction debris, which was still sitting in our driveway from when Joe had remodeled the second floor. I wasn't sure how I'd find the energy to do it myself. Kyle also told me that more of our coworkers had come to support me, but they didn't know what to say and were still outside.

While I barely noticed the people who were coming and going that day, something about Kyle's visit seeped into my consciousness. Here was someone who wasn't afraid to see the grief on my face or uncomfortable looking me in the eye. It was as if a small light had filtered into the darkness surrounding me. At that moment, I knew Kyle was someone who had survived the darkness, someone who knew it could be conquered and wanted to share that knowledge, that fleck of light, with me. And he did, not by offering sympathy or words of comfort, but by acknowledging that grief made people uncomfortable, showing he wasn't afraid of it. His desire to support me in my grief was stronger than any discomfort he may have felt.

THE DAY AFTER JOE died, Wade had his two-week checkup. His doctor called and offered to make a house call, but I declined. I didn't want to inconvenience him. But more than that, I hoped to find out what the doctors who examined Joe had found. At some point during the night, the police had informed us that they no longer thought it was a hit-and-run. Still, I wanted to know what they had seen with the benefit of light.

There was one other reason I wanted to bring Wade to the clinic. I was afraid that something would be wrong with him. I was afraid that I couldn't take care of him and keep him alive on my own, afraid of the unknown and the future.

Wade's checkup went well, though. He was healthy, thriving, and gaining weight from nursing. But that didn't ease my doubts that I could do it alone. All the confidence I had felt with Joe by my side was gone the instant he died. In a way, it wasn't logical that so much of my belief and confidence in myself was tied to Joe and his belief in me. No matter where he was, he still believed in me. But emotionally speaking, I couldn't convince myself of it.

That night, when I finally went to bed, I walked into the room and stood there. I hadn't been in that bed since the last time Joe had been there with me; and even with something so simple, I wasn't sure what to do. How could I lie down on this mattress that was no longer welcoming and comforting? That no longer resembled the bed I knew and loved because the person I knew and loved was no longer a part of it? Plus, neither Joe nor I had our own sides anymore. The entire bed was mine alone, and it didn't matter that I didn't want it.

Eventually, I lay down on Joe's side of the bed. That was the closest I could get to him. So I lay where he had lain and showered where he had showered. I wore his deodorant and cried where no one could see or hear me. Even though I was surrounded by friends and family who loved Joe and were there to support me as we grieved over the man we'd known and loved in our own ways, I had never felt more alone in my life. Light and warmth had left my world.

I couldn't make sense of what had happened in the last twenty-four hours. It was inconceivable that Joe had just died. The only logical conclusion I could come to was that someone had hit him late at night on that dark road. What else could it have been? Joe was only thirty years old. He was healthy and athletic. So I clung to the fact that someone had done this to him, that this must have been a hit-and-run. The idea gave me someone to blame.

Still, as the police concluded their investigation, they determined no foul play was involved. The coroner completed the autopsy and ruled that Joe had died of unknown natural causes. I had wanted to blame someone, to point and scream at them and tell them they ruined our lives and were horrible people. But there was no one to blame for Joe's death, no one to blame for my inability to save him and for God not answering my prayers.

I wanted that anger, though. I could understand that more than sadness and loss. I could navigate that emotion, whereas the others made me feel adrift. Sadness scared me, because it ran to my core and I didn't know how to overcome it. I also feared the darkness that came again with the sadness; and while Joe had pulled me out of it after the miscarriages, he wasn't here to pull me out this time. I feared I'd spend the rest of my life blindly groping around in the dark, trying to piece my life back together and failing to do so.

So, for a while, I chose anger. It was safer at the time. Eventually I learned that anger is OK, but hanging on to anger can make you bitter and jealous. That was what happened to me, because I believed it wasn't fair and I deserved what others had. And the bitterness and jealousy began to strip me of my humanity.

I spent days sitting in Joe's chair, feeding or rocking Wade whenever someone handed him to me, and staring blindly at the TV while my insides swirled with abandonment, disbelief, anger, and resentment. Family and friends dropped everything to help with cooking, cleaning, answering the phone, informing other relatives about Joe's death, and arranging any benefits and bereavement paperwork I needed to complete for my and Joe's employer. They only penetrated my darkness and numb stares when I needed to make the most important decisions.

Yet even in my grief, I was a planner, and I wanted the control. Joe had been my husband. It was important that I make the decisions about his burial and memorial service. I didn't want to, but what I wanted was no longer realistic. And I didn't want anyone to make those decisions for me. My need to maintain control helped me shake off the fog and numbness I had been living in since I had found Joe's body. I was able to function, but only when I needed to make his final arrangements.

One of the questions I needed to answer was where to bury Joe. At first, it seemed obvious. Burns has only one cemetery. And when we had done our wills, Joe had said that if he had to be buried there, he wanted to be buried by his grandma. However, he had also said he wished he could be buried at the ranch.

This was one of those times when being surrounded by friends and family was an unexpected benefit. When I told them what was in Joe's will, someone picked up on the nuance in my answer and asked where Joe had really wanted to be buried. So I told them the truth. He had preferred open spaces, and the ranch was where he felt calmness, happiness, and peace. We hadn't written this in the will because we had assumed there were rules against it. And even then, days after Joe had died, I still assumed a burial at the ranch wouldn't be allowed.

At that point, someone in the room mentioned that all we had to do was go to the courthouse and register a plot of land on the ranch as a cemetery. The fact that it was possible to bury Joe in the place he loved most, the place he considered home, brought me some comfort. I could do little for him now that he was dead, and realizing I could do this for him gave me a small feeling of control. It wasn't much, but in that moment it was enough.

After that, we finished making Joe's final arrangements. His dad, brother, and grandfather determined the best location on the ranch. Someone else worked with the courthouse. My dad, who wasn't too familiar with the town of Burns, told me he would go back home to the welding shop he ran with my brother and sister, make a fence for the cemetery, and ensure it was installed before Joe's service. He found a way to support me that meant more than him just sitting near me, unsure what to say; and I loved him more for it.

People buzzed around me, filling their day with activities to prepare for Joe's memorial service. In the meantime, I sat in Joe's recliner, staring at nothing and frozen in the shock of darkness. I

held on to our baby and tried to breathe, but that was more difficult than I thought it would be.

Some part of me knew that I had Cody and Wade, and I had
to survive for them. But survival seemed too hard. So I let the
numbness take over, drank the smoothies my sister brought me
(solid food was making me sick at the time), and prayed this wasn't
my life.

Somehow, in the midst of all this, I planned Joe's memorial
service. Memories of seeing my great-grandma in her open casket
reminded me that I didn't want the last image people would have
of Joe to be him lying in an open casket. Instead, I wanted them to
remember how he was when he was full of life. So I decided that
Joe's service would be open to the public, with a private burial the
following day for family and friends.

I also tried to figure out how I could honor Joe and show how
much I loved him, and how I could live without him. So I wrote
his obituary, a poem for the program, and a speech for the service.
I designed his gravestone, all the while wishing I could just be
wherever he was.

Don't get me wrong—I didn't really want to die. I just didn't
want to live, which isn't the same as being suicidal. Despite this,
I knew one thing for certain: Joe would want me to live. It was
as simple as that. He always told me he had no regrets, and I was
sure he felt that way even in death. He would have wanted me
to carry on, and I'd have to figure out how to save myself on the
memories I held dear and the love that still existed in my heart and
his, wherever he was.

That was what I needed to figure out: how to to carry on, for
Joe and for the boys. Hanging onto anger so I wouldn't have to
feel anything wasn't the answer. For the first time, as I was writing

words I hoped would honor Joe and support his legacy, I forced myself to think, remember, and feel.

It hurt, and tears streaked down my face until I had cried myself out. But I also felt my first glimmers of calm, peace, and happiness—or at least a reminder of those feelings. I was learning that I could create some light in this darkness. I could do it myself, and Joe would help through my memories and love for him, which could never be taken from me. Joe had left a legacy on my heart, and I needed to share that with the people who would come to honor him, despite my shyness and hatred of public speaking. I wanted to make him proud.

When the day of Joe's service arrived, our neighbor's wife came to do my hair. I had no idea who arranged it, but I was thankful they did. I was three weeks postpartum, my husband had died, and I couldn't breathe. To be honest, looking like a normal human being at his service wasn't high on my list of priorities. In fact, I didn't have much of a list, other than surviving, breathing, and getting through the next few days without collapsing in a ball onto the floor. Yet the comfort of knowing I'd at least appear presentable, even if I only stood in front of everyone and cried, left a little of my dignity intact.

We were ushered into a small room in the building that was hosting Joe's service, while close to five hundred people gathered in the other room. I thought then that this was it. After the service and the next day, the day of Joe's burial, I would be alone. I would be a widow at the age of thirty-one and wishing I were the one who was gone instead. So I panicked. I had no idea how I'd get through the service. And since God and I still weren't on speaking terms, I couldn't find any comfort there.

I clenched Wade tightly to me. His blue-and-white blanket was wrapped around him, providing both of us with some much-needed warmth. Then I leaned on Joe's brother, and we walked to our seats. Those who'd come to remember Joe stopped talking, leaving only the muffled sounds of grief throughout the room and the ear-shattering cries in my soul that threatened to break free.

I sat as the service began, led by the pastor who had married Joe and me not quite five years earlier. A friend of the family gave Joe's eulogy. It took everything I had to keep from shaking out of my skin, from running away and leaving this all behind. But I didn't. I stayed there and listened to the eulogy.

And then it was my turn. I passed Wade off to Joe's brother and climbed the stairs to the podium without falling, clutched its sides as tightly as I could to keep from crumpling into a ball and giving into the darkness. Then I read what I had prepared to honor Joe.

I told the other mourners about my husband, though most of them were already familiar with what I shared. Joe had wanted to leave a legacy for Cody and Wade, and he had planned to do it throughout what he had hoped would be a long life. But I wanted it to be clear that despite his short time on earth, Joe had still left a legacy. He had wanted to make sure his boys grew up with that lifestyle and learned strong morals, good manners, and a diligent work ethic. He had also wanted to leave a mark on the community where he had grown up and loved enough to raise his own kids. He hadn't thought he had achieved that yet, but as I looked around the room during my speech, I remarked that it was obvious he had made a much bigger mark than he could have ever fathomed.

At the same time, I thought Joe would have actually hated that so many people had taken time out of their busy lives to come to his service, and yet he would have felt so honored, blessed, and humbled by it. He was a great man, full of life, dreams, and plans designed with family in mind. It wouldn't be easy, but I made up my mind then and there to make as many of those dreams come true as possible; and I would do it with love and strength because Joe had given me both. So I vowed before the other mourners that I wouldn't give up and that we'd always remember and love Joe. He couldn't have left a better legacy.

After the service, someone brought Cody to the potluck. (I had chosen not to bring him to the service, since I thought it would be too hard for such a young child to see the raw emotion of loss on so many faces.) I watched him play while Wade was passed around, and I was overwhelmed with hugs. So many people wanted to show their support and love by embracing us. But since I had never been a very touchy-feely person, I stood stiffly, with my arms at my sides, as most of the mourners who had attended the service offered their condolences . . . and hugs. So many hugs, in fact, that I eventually grew numb to them.

While I appreciated the condolences (and, somewhat less, the hugs), what meant the most to me was the amazing presence of all the people who had come. The support that the other mourners poured out to me—regardless of whether they had known me, Joe, or both of us—left me in awe. One person who specifically stood out was the mom of a childhood friend who had traveled two hours to the service. I hadn't been close with her daughter since elementary school, but that didn't matter. I was truly touched that she was there, reaching out and offering support because she felt she needed to, without fearing whether it was awkward or proper.

THE NEXT DAY, WE buried Joe.

In the morning, I went to the chapel with the boys, my family, and Joe's family and met with other loved ones who joined the procession to Joe's final resting place. Before we left the chapel, we were given the option to see him.

I didn't want to see Joe's body, and I felt so guilty about that. Shouldn't I want to see him one last time? But as far as I was concerned, he was gone. He had already left me, and only his used flesh and bones were in that box. Everything that had made Joe who he was had left for the heavens over a week earlier.

Still, some of his family and mine wanted to see him. So we took turns going in, saying our goodbyes. I watched his dad go up to his son's body and thought, *This isn't how it should be.* His dad slipped something into the casket before he left.

Then it was my turn. The knot in my stomach tightened, and the tentacles of grief waving around inside brought a flush of warmth and numbness that I'd need to sustain myself. I walked up to Joe's simple pine box and looked down at the man I had loved—or, rather, the man I still loved and would always love— and I knew everything I was, and everything I had become with Joe by my side, would be buried with him. The life I had known was over and now somewhere in that casket, with my husband. The woman who stood there, in the dimly lit chapel, was only a shell of my former self.

I slipped a photo and a letter under Joe's hand. They weren't for him, since he was dead, but for me. They were reminders of all we'd had, all we'd loved, and all we'd planned. Then I took one last look at him and tried not to laugh hysterically at how he would hate wearing so much makeup. He looked as I remembered, with some postmortem foundation and rouge. But it still wasn't him. There's so much more to a person than their looks. Their essence, their soul, or whatever you want to call it—that makes a person who they are. And what I saw in the casket wasn't my husband. He was already gone. No feeling of him was there in the chapel, just as there hadn't been on the side of the road the night I had found him.

The time had come then. I stood by and watched while Joe's brother and the other pallbearers loaded Joe into the back of the truck that he had built, the old red GMC with the Cummins diesel engine he had installed. It had been a dream project for the last few years, and now it would give him his last ride. I rode in the passenger seat while his brother drove. Looking back on it now, though, it was all so surreal that I might have floated above the truck and seen the same view Joe must have seen.

As a final honor, Joe was escorted by a number of wildland fire engines sporting American flags as if they were in a parade. And they were: it was Joe's final parade.

We laid Joe to rest at the foot of a small hill on the ranch, overlooking the meadows he loved. They were brown in winter, but they would be lush, green, and filled with purple camas in the spring and grazed calmly by his beloved cows in the summer. One of Joe's close friends played his guitar and sang "Amarillo by Morning," Joe's favorite song.

Words were said, flowers were dropped on the casket, and then it was over. Everyone else streamed out of the small, newly established cemetery; and I was left to say goodbye alone.

I have no idea how long I stood there. There were no tears this time, though. I had none left in me. I just stood there, for a few seconds or an eternity. Time held no meaning. I cried out and talked to him quietly—or perhaps it was all in my head. I wondered if anyone would notice if I crawled down in that grave with him and if I could get away with it; and for a few minutes, I lived in that fantasy. I grabbed at my heart as I felt it break even more, the tiny pieces shattering into slivers. The tangible pain reminded me I wasn't dead or dying. I was alive, alone, and in the darkness of grief. I was a shell of a person, now living a life no one would ask for yet one I wouldn't give up.

I wouldn't give up my life because, like Joe had said, I had no regrets and I would pick him and this heartache a million times over. (The saying, "No regrets," was eventually engraved on his gravestone.) I would hang on and learn to live again, if not for myself then for our sons. Again I made Joe that silent promise, brushed the dirt from my pants, and walked away while he was covered with six feet of earth.

I didn't know it then, but from my grief I'd grow into a new person with a new life. Shadows and pieces of that old me would still be present, but they would be pieced back together with new pieces made from grief. It would be up to me. I would have to choose how I grew into that shell, molded by tragedy.

7

S OMETIME AFTER JOE WAS BURIED, I got a message from a friend. His brother, a local cowboy and musician named Levi Harris, had attended Joe's memorial service and was moved to write a song about Joe called "Smilin' at Me." The song had been written from the heart, and it showed in the lyrics. It also captured Joe's essence and the things he loved and valued. Listening to the song immediately brought tears to my eyes and a smile to my face, so vivid was the picture of Joe "smilin' at me" from his vantage point in heaven. Once the song was recorded on CD, I was able to listen to other songs Levi had written. Many of the songs were about loss, but from the perspective of living after loss. There was hope in the music, a little ray of light into the darkness given to me by a stranger.

After the funeral, friends and family headed back home. Now that the task of burying my husband was done, I was struggling in my own skin, fighting to escape the darkness. I knew there was a way, but I was unsure of the path. In my grief, I wanted nothing more than to leave it all behind: my friends and family who grieved with me and wanted to help but didn't know how; all the pitying looks, sympathy, and condolences; the responsibilities, dogs, and kids. I loved my sons, but in my core I wanted the freedom to grieve as I wished, without the fear and the worry of what others would think and the pressure of helping others grieve. I needed to focus on myself. I needed to cry somewhere other than in the shower. I needed to be alone so I could cry, think, and just be.

I was ashamed that I wanted to run. I had promised Joe that I'd take care of our boys, and I felt like I was letting him down by indulging in the fantasy of leaving for Italy or Greece and finding a small cottage where I could live in peace and quiet and no one would know my story or speak my language. If I felt alone, why not be alone? There was something alluring about matching my external situation with how I felt inside. But while I dreamed, I knew I'd never do it. I loved my boys and my family, and I would never leave them. Yet I also knew on some level that I needed to run away, at least for a little bit. I needed some time to try to find my way. To find the light and the good that were left for me in the world.

I had a responsibility, and I wouldn't be able to fulfill it while I felt tied down. I needed to be alone, truly alone, for the first time since Joe had died. I needed to figure out how to live with this loss and create a new life from the wreckage I was left with, and I needed to do this alone. I didn't want to be watched with pity or concern, and I wasn't worried about making others feel uncomfortable. So I arranged to go to the coast for a few days. My mom made a hotel reservation for a room on the beach, with a kitchen so I wouldn't have to have to go out to eat if I didn't want to. She packed food for my trip and agreed to stay at my house and take care of Cody and Wade while I was gone.

Alone, I drove the seven hours to Bandon, a small town on the Pacific coast. I rented a small room where I could see and hear the ocean, with a fridge for the breast milk I'd pump every three hours. The hotel was also close to Shore Acres State Park, which I had visited years before. Now I was drawn back, even though Joe and I had never gone there together.

Shore Acres featured five acres of formal gardens that were

originally designed in the early 1900s by Louis J. Simpson, a lumberman and shipbuilder who brought hundreds of plants from all over the world for his estate. That was where I spent most of my time at the park, wandering aimlessly for hours. No one talked to me or asked me questions. Few visitors were there despite the unseasonably warm weather. I was free to do what I wanted. I could stop and sit on the edge of one garden, think or read for a bit, then get up and find another inviting corner of another.

What I liked most about the formal gardens was that they were organized and controlled. Flower beds were edged with shrubs, with straight paths leading between them. There was a peace in knowing there would be no surprises except maybe an early tulip in bloom. I felt the calming sensation of things being under control and going exactly as planned. Even in the gardens' rigid structure, there was peace and beauty.

On the edge of the formal garden was a Japanese-style garden with a small lily pond, an area that was suggestive of a poem. This garden was created to be calming, peaceful, and a little wild, a place where suffering was OK because it was a part of existence. It was a place where brokenness mixed with peace and beauty because in nature it all goes hand in hand.

I made my way around the lily pond and climbed the rock steps to a dirt path that wound through the evergreen trees and opened into a small meadow where dozens of rose bushes were planted. Their stems were bare except for some thorns and a few new leaf buds. As I wandered slowly around the rose bushes, I felt the sun on my back and saw it reflecting on the new buds. For a few moments, I was able to step out of the darkness, feel the warmth of the day on my skin, and accept the fact that, even without Joe, the sun still rose. Life was still all around me. It was just up to me to find it. On that February day in those gardens, I saw firsthand how life was sprouting out of the darkness of winter and growing from the small seeds of last year's plants. Each new flower would be a little different from its predecessor, but no less beautiful. I wanted to be like those flowers.

Outside the formal gardens were paths that meandered through the coastal forest. One narrow trail in particular led down the bluff to a small hidden cove. Here, the cliffs of the coastline suddenly broke, showing a narrow opening between the rocks that let the ocean waves calmly wash up on the isolated beach. I was the only person on that beach, and the solitude gave me comfort. No one was watching me. It was just me, sand, and cliffs looking out to the vast ocean. The cliffs surrounding the beach protected it from the elements, turning it into a small pocket of peace in the rush of wind and waves. I sat there and rubbed my hand on the coarse sand, drawing patterns, smoothing them over, and letting the tranquility of the moment settle over me.

After a while, a family made their way down to the beach. So I climbed up the path, noticing for the first time a small creek that was partially hidden in the undergrowth. I followed the path as it wove back through the forest and along the edge of gardens. The forest opened into a clearing up on the bluffs where a mansion used to overlook the moody blue-gray waves of the Pacific Ocean. I wandered past benches and a small observation building before heading into the other side of the forest. After a few hundred feet, the path led into another clearing. I saw the remnants of a tennis court, slowly crumbling to nature as the waves eroded the sandstone cliffs. When I reached the top of the bluff, I watched the waves below me take out their fury on the rocks. As they crashed against the cliff, they would explode into the air like white fireworks. Drops of water landed feet away from where I stood. It was a beautiful display of nature's power.

I stood there, amazed at the beauty of something so simple as waves wreaking havoc on the rocks. Here, I felt the turmoil in my soul. And like the waves releasing their power, I started to let go of my anger at Joe for leaving me, God for not saving him, and the world for everything else. I stood there and screamed, and the roar of the ocean drowned out the noise I made. With each shattering wave, I let go of some of my anger. Not all of it and not for forever, but it was a start. I knew I was angry and had been keeping that emotion to myself. But there on the cliffs, I gave it free rein to erupt from me like the water below. I realized how much holding on to anger had been tearing me apart, eroding parts of my soul that were trying to heal as it bounced around inside me. I knew then that I needed to figure out how to let the rest of my anger go.

I stayed on that sandstone bluff until I felt tired and drained of anger. Then I went back to the overlook and found a bench where I could continue watching the rolling ocean and listen to the water hitting the rocks below. There I sat for hours, watching the waves roll across an infinite abyss. On occasion I'd read *The Sun Still Rises: Surviving and Thriving After Grief,* a book by Shawn Doyle that I had brought with me. My dad had picked it out for me right after Joe died because he "felt" it would be the right one. In this book, Doyle discusses the loss of his wife as well as his personal experiences with grief. He shares the lessons he learned, such as how sometimes there are just no answers. He also presents myths about grief, including how people think they know how you feel but in fact don't, because no one else has lived your life or felt your loss.

When I had the energy to read *The Sun Still Rises*, I devoured the information it provided, but one quote in particular stood out to me. Toward the end of the book, I read these lines: "Every day the sun still rises. You can either turn and face it, or hide in the dark." These words describe so perfectly how I had been feeling while wandering around Shore Acres. The feeling that the sunlight could help me heal, and that I'd find more comfort in the light than in wrapping myself in anger and sadness. The light seemed much more inviting than hiding in the dark, avoiding a life that wasn't what I had planned it to be. Reading that book at Shore Acres allowed me to see that hope was possible

After I finished reading, I was tired of the gardens. So I wandered back down to the beach and sat on the sand again, feeling its coarseness, softness, and warmth beneath me. I laid back against the cold, smooth stone of the cliffs, marveling at the contrasts of life and wondering if, like nature, I could grow from my grief. Could I embrace spring and let myself piece my heart and soul back together? Could I rebuild myself into something new yet similar to who I was before? Could I still be happy despite wearing the inevitable scars of trauma? I didn't know how exactly I would do any of this. But Doyle's book had given me some ideas, and I wanted to act on them by making choices that promoted healing. I could control my choices.

While I felt empty without Joe in my life, I wasn't truly empty. Deep within me, I still had life, love, memories, and—most importantly—hope. It was all just below the surface, hidden out of sight, and I had to look for it. The ocean gave me a certain comfort that no one had been able to give me yet. It gave me peace, and I imagined that somewhere out there, across the giant expanse, was Joe. For me, the ocean became a symbol of the chasm dividing life and death. And sitting on that bench, looking into the chasm, I felt closer to Joe.

Before, when I was writing the speech for his service, I knew what Joe would tell me. But for the first time since before he had died, I felt him standing behind me, his arms wrapping around me as we stood on the bluff. His voice whispered in my ear, telling me that it was OK, that I was strong and just needed to trust my-self, that he loved me always and forever, just as he had so many times before. He was in my heart and in my memories. I wasn't really alone. Because I had loved Joe and he had loved me, he would always be with me.

When I got up to leave, I felt a lightness. My legs didn't feel so heavy as I stretched and looked out at the ocean. As I turned to go, I picked up a stick and wrote Joe's name in the sand. That way, anyone who would see it would know he had been there.

At Shore Acres, I had found something that matched what I felt; then, what I felt changed. Watching the empty ocean play upon the shore made me realize it wasn't truly empty. Instead, it was full of life, animals, and plants, just as the gardens at Shore Acres seemed dead but were just dormant, with some life begin-ning to bloom. I just hadn't been able to see it on the surface. What's unexpected wasn't necessarily bad. In nature, as in life, there is always death and birth, suffering and happiness. These concepts are always together, since one isn't possible without the other. And similarly, without love, there is no loss. The cost of love is loss and grief. And the thing is, the cost of love is so high that it's impossible to realize it until you suffer that loss.

Shore Acres was the escape I needed, a place that matched my soul. No matter what I was feeling, I was able to find some com-fort there. There I found Joe again and knew I'd keep him with me always, in my heart and memories. It was there that I also learned it was OK to cry for him while smiling at his memory despite the tears. It was OK to feel and live. I knew this precious feeling of peace and confidence wouldn't last, but I was happy to know it at least existed. That knowledge would make it easier to return to this peace, and to hold on to hope, if I were to lose it again.

8

WHEN I RETURNED HOME FROM my week in Bandon, I found that most of my relatives had left. My mom, however, had arranged with her employer to stay with me as long as I needed her. I hadn't asked her to stay, but she had seen I was barely able to take care of myself. I still wasn't sure how to do it, either, despite my discoveries at Shore Acres. I was tired all the time and had no appetite. I was forgetful and only able to focus on what was necessary, like taking care of Cody and Wade. Still, my mom was doing most of that work. She gave me time while I struggled with depression and tried to figure out how to live my new life.

My mom stayed for almost two months. At first she let me be, so I did as little as possible, which still felt like too much to handle sometimes. I was a shell of a person, wandering around and doing my best to not face the truth. I didn't want to; I wanted my life back. Without Joe, I didn't know who or what I was or what my plans for the future were. I didn't want to survive this, though I knew I would, if for no other reason than the boys. I didn't want to thrive, and I didn't see how I could without accepting that Joe had died or forgetting what we'd had and what I had lost. But since that was impossible, how would I ever be OK with the fact that he died? I would never forget our love and how great we were together. So how would it be possible to really live life?

While at the coast, I had felt at peace and thought I could

survive and even learn to be happy again. But that feeling became harder to find when I returned to the real world. It was harder to hold onto, harder to believe. It was constantly lost in the face of reality, the fog of grief, and the fear of doing it all alone.

In the first six weeks or so after Joe died, I lost all my pregnancy weight and then some. Nothing tasted good, and the effort it took me to chew, swallow, and digest food was exhausting. If I did eat, either I would feel nauseous or my stomach would hurt until the food worked its way through my system. Some people may find comfort in eating when dealing with grief and loss. But for me, this simple, life-sustaining action felt foreign. It didn't feel right to eat when Joe couldn't. He had loved to eat everything, and he would eat a lot. So every time I was given food, I'd wonder what Joe would think of it.

I felt awful that I wasn't eating. And I knew I needed to, if I was going to breastfeed Wade. My sons were all I had left, but I knew I wouldn't be able to take care of them for long at the rate I was losing weight.

At one point, someone in my family gave me what they considered a compliment: "You look great. You've lost a lot of weight."

I thought, Really? Are you serious? You know I'm not eating. You've been watching them feed me smoothies because that's all I can handle. I wanted to say, "Yeah, husbands dying make for a great diet." Instead, I just said, "Thank you."

Afterward, I thought it was good that I didn't suffer from an eating disorder. I was depressed, weak, and tired. But to at least one person, I looked better than I ever had. This was only a few weeks after Joe's death and Wade's birth. It seemed like I was being rewarded for being unhealthy, for starving myself. I couldn't help but wonder why our society believes this kind of "compliment" could make people feel better. No wonder so many people battle unhealthy habits with food when those habits continue to be encouraged.

This was the first time I realized that people have no idea what to say when you're grieving. I had noticed before that grief made people uncomfortable, to the point that they would avoid someone who was grieving. But this statement made it clear that, while some people want to help and provide comfort, our society does nothing to prepare people for those moments.

Other residents in Burns started a meal train for me. Every day, someone would bring us a complete meal. The freezer began to fill up, and the three of us barely made a dent in each meal. Eventually, we requested to get only three meals per week. I both appreciated and hated the meal train. Even though I wasn't eating or taking care of my kids, just knowing that food was available for us to reheat was a blessing. Plus, it was one less thing my mom had to do and one less thing I had to ask of her. But while it was a comfort, I also hated the attention. I didn't want people to waste their time taking care of me. Nor did I want them to know I needed it or that I wasn't functioning. I wanted them to see me as the strong woman who, when her husband died, would grit her teeth and pull herself up by her bootstraps to do what needed to be done.

On the other hand, I didn't want them to tell me how strong I was. I felt broken, and being told I was strong seemed like a lie. It was just a phrase people would say when you're grieving in an effort to make you feel better. I felt weaker than I ever had before, like I could barely stand. And I knew those words were meant to comfort me, but they fell flat.

Much later, I learned you can be strong and feel weak at the same time. The feelings aren't mutually exclusive, and in my case I had to be strong just to survive this tragedy. I didn't know yet that being strong when grieving doesn't mean you don't cry or aren't able to do the things you did before your loss. Rather, being strong in grief is just surviving being hit by a bus of emotions and eventually figuring out how to live after losing everything you thought you knew and were. That is true strength, and I can look back on that time in my life now and know I was strong even though I didn't feel that way.

My mom and I settled into a routine. I would wake up and feed Wade, and she would do everything else for him and Cody. Then we'd drop Cody off at daycare, and she would drive me around to help me take care of finishing things related to Joe's death. Later, we'd pick up Cody and go home, where I'd pretend to eat dinner, she would get the boys ready for bed, I'd say goodnight, and we'd go to bed.

Eventually, as I expected, my weight loss was enough that I couldn't keep feeding Wade. I couldn't eat more, so I switched Wade to formula. I felt a lot of guilt over that decision, but I'm not sure why. Maybe it was because I had breastfed Cody for a full year, and now I wasn't giving Wade the time and attention he deserved. But we also live in a culture that currently thinks breast-feeding is better and "shames" women who don't. Switching Wade to formula to ensure he was getting the nutrients he needed was the best I could do at the time, but it took me a while to realize my best was still enough.

ON SUNDAYS, MY MOM would take us to church. I felt more anger and pain while sitting in church than anywhere else. I was so angry at God for allowing Joe to die so young. Church felt like hell; none of the peace I used to feel while sitting in the pew was there. I couldn't find comfort in a faith that tells its believers that there's a reason for everything, that miracles can happen. But a miracle hadn't happened for me the night Joe died, and I wouldn't forget it. Sitting in church reminded me that the thousands of prayers I made as I kneeled in the gravel next to Joe, gave him CPR, and watched while the EMTs worked on him went unanswered. So I would sit there quietly, tears running silently down my face, trying not to scream and yell and throw a fit. If anyone had deserved a miracle, it was Joe.

At that point, I didn't understand why a place where so many people find comfort was the last place I wanted to be. So while I felt angry and hurt, I also felt ashamed and guilty. What right did I have to be angry at God? It didn't help that some members of the congregation who knew me or Joe, or at least knew what had happened, would ask, "How are you doing?" A number of them would even tell me that Joe's death "happened for a reason," or that it was all part of "God's plan" and Joe was "in a better place."

No one wants to hear that God plans things that way, though. I didn't want to hear that God had planned for me to lose my husband and myself, and for our boys to grow up without a dad who loved them so much. Maybe people were trying to show me there was a silver lining. But it wasn't helpful, especially so early in my grief. I was so raw that even the idea of a silver lining hurt. How can there be anything good out of such a loss? I only saw the pain I felt. When I looked toward the future, I only imagined that pain carrying forward, as sharp and overwhelming as it was at that time. I couldn't see any comfort in the good that could be found in Joe's death.

I didn't talk to anyone about my anger at God, but someone noticed. I don't remember who; the fog of grief left many gaps in my memory. But I do remember what they said, because it worked its way into my heart and mind, like a sliver of light penetrating the darkness: "It's OK to be angry with God. He not only understands, but He expects it. We don't have to be perfect; we are not perfect. He is perfect. He understands that just because this may be part of His plan, it doesn't mean it was part of yours. God can handle your anger."

This was one of the most helpful pieces of advice I received early in my grieving. It showed me there was no need to be ashamed or guilty for being angry with God. It was also the first time that I was given permission to "feel my feelings," and the first time someone told me something that didn't seem like a platitude. This advice wasn't a shallow attempt to make me feel better. Instead, it was a real attempt to reach me, to help me. The speaker gave me permission to grieve, and therefore gave me the most comfort. Feeling my feelings was more painful at that moment, but it was a lot easier than always fighting them.

A FEW WEEKS AFTER Joe died, one of our friends called. I wasn't very close with the woman or her family, but Joe had fought fire with her husband and become good friends with him. The friend had tickets for a local event and asked if I wanted to go. Well, she didn't ask. Rather, she said she had a ticket for me to go with them and told me when they would pick me up. The conversation may not have gone exactly that way, but it left me with the impression it would just be easier to say yes. Close friends didn't just offer help or wait for me to ask. Instead, they told me what they were going to do for me and when, then dared me to refuse. It was just as difficult for me to turn down help as it was to ask for it, so in the end I let them help me.

I didn't want to go. I hated going anywhere. I hated the looks of pity and the recognition I'd receive when running errands in Burns. One time, I even went to a different gas station than usual. When the attendant came to my window, I said, "Fill it up regular, please," and handed him my credit card.

He read the name on the credit card and froze. "Toelle?" he asked, still looking at the card. "Was that your husband who just died?"

"Yes," I replied, trying to keep the frustration out of my voice. How was it possible that people recognized who I was no matter where I went? All I wanted was to get gas and pretend everything was normal for a few minutes.

"Oh man, I'm so sorry," the attendant said. "What a horrible thing. He just died? Do they know why?" He was finally looking up at me.

"No. He just died," I said, sounding flat and tired.

"Crazy," he said, shaking his head. "Regular, you said?"

In our small town, everyone had heard what had happened. I hated it even when I was driving somewhere, feeling those stares of recognition. So I drove my mom's car instead of mine as often as possible. I hated being a "celebrity" in Burns, but that was what I felt like. It was impossible to go anywhere and pretend, even for ten minutes, that my husband wasn't dead. There was no opportunity for denial for me. I was forced to be in my grief, no matter what.

It didn't really matter where I went, since I likely would have been recognized. So I called my friend and told her I would go. At the event, I sat with her, her husband, and other friends of mine and Joe's. A few hundred people were there, eating dinner and participating in raffles and a silent auction. I probably wasn't much fun to be around that night, but my friends weren't expecting that. They just wanted to show me I wasn't alone, that I had friends who could look my grief in the face. As I sat there at our table, keeping to myself, I didn't feel pressured to contribute to their conversation. But neither did I feel like they were avoiding conversation with me. When they asked me a question, they wouldn't just glance at me. They would look in my eyes and not recoil if they saw tears there.

More than once, when I felt like I was struggling to keep myself from crying, the friend who had invited me would quietly ask, "Do you need to leave? It's OK if you do."

"No, I'll be OK. I just need a minute," I'd say, wiping tears from my eyes.

"Can I get you anything?" she asked another time.

"No, thank you," I replied.

While the words were simple, how they made me feel was not. I felt that I was seen. She didn't look away when she saw tears in my eyes, and my tears were reflected in her eyes. I didn't feel like my grief made her awkward. She offered comfort but listened to what I said. She didn't try to force anything upon me or act like she knew what was best.

Her and her husband's reactions to me and my grief reminded me that they grieved too. They didn't mourn in the same way I did, but they were able to relate to my mourning. They made an effort to be there for me, without overwhelming me with pity or discomfort. Even though we were in Burns, they seemed to be a shield, protecting me from my unwanted fame and treating me as a normal person. How they acted toward me that night meant more to me than the hundreds of condolences and offers of help I had received since Joe had died.

In the end, that friend and her husband became two of the few people I felt comfortable asking for help, which I learned to do out of necessity. I still value their friendship deeply and know they'll be there for me, no matter what I need. In turn, I've done my best to support them whenever I can. Most importantly, I've never forgotten how they truly meant it when they offered help and said they would be there for me, and I'll always appreciate that more than I can ever say.

9

A FEW MONTHS BEFORE JOE died, he had asked me what I really wanted out of life. We were sitting together on the living room couch, looking out the window at the hay field and the valley below. He watched me intently while he waited for my answer. Eventually, I said that I didn't know, that I felt like I already had what I wanted: an amazing husband, one kid with another on the way, the chance to be a great wife and mom, a job I didn't hate, travel opportunities, and a place where the man I loved and I could grow old together.

We sat in silence for a minute. I had never really thought about what I wanted out of life, and I wasn't sure how else to answer. Yet my answer hadn't satisfied Joe. He just looked at me, his brown eyes soft, and said, "No, that doesn't count." What he wanted to know was what I wanted to do just for myself, to give myself that full satisfaction with life. He didn't want me to feel like I had given up anything, or to settle for a family and give up on hopes and dreams I was holding quietly in my heart. He wanted me to be completely fulfilled.

Joe said he knew what he wanted: to be a rancher. He wanted to have his own cows and do all the work that went along with it, including all-night calving, branding, doctoring, feeding, marketing, breeding, and selling. He wanted to work all on his own, have the final say, make the final decisions, and experiment with ways to improve his operations without debating his ideas with other people. He also wanted to use ranching as a way to teach his kids about caring for animals, working hard, and living with the great outdoors. Joe's face lit up as he told me all of this. He became excited and animated, and I wanted to do whatever I could to help him make his dreams a reality.

Still, I didn't have a great answer for myself. The most I came up with was to get a new horse that was young enough to ride and compete. (Norman had been retired and was living out the rest of his life in the pasture.) Riding was the one thing I had ever excelled at, and it gave me a sense of pride, peace, calm, and comfort I hadn't found elsewhere. While my answer wasn't as complete as Joe's, it satisfied him for the moment. We then spent the rest of the evening going over our finances, trying to figure out where we could cut costs, save money, and move in the direction of our dreams.

Horses and cows were expensive. But since Joe's family had a ranch, it was possible that he could give up his day job as an engineer. We could survive on my income, and Joe could work at the ranch full-time, as long as he could make $500 a month. We agreed we would give it one more year with two incomes, create a safety net, and save some money to buy a horse before he quit his day job.

Sadly, we never got that chance. But I hope that knowing we were working toward his dream, and that his dreams were important to me, was enough for Joe.

WHILE MY FIRST ANSWER about wanting to be a wife and mom wasn't what Joe had been looking for, it was still true. So once he died, I found I no longer felt like a wife. After all, where was my husband? I also couldn't bring myself out of my grief enough to feel like a great mom. Instead, I was minimally engaged with my boys. Though I felt confident in who I was as an individual before Joe had died, I lacked that confidence afterward. So much of what I had felt about myself and known myself to be had been wrapped up in being his wife.

Who was I now?

Life had molded me into the person I had become, and some part of me realized what I'd become with Joe would now have to be shaped into what I would be after Joe. Initially I didn't know how to make that change. My mom, however, gave me the only gift possible: time to figure out who I would be without the heavy responsibility of sole parenthood I had been thrust into.

Slowly she passed back to me some of my responsibilities, starting with Cody's bedtime ritual, which included reading books, prayers, hugs, and kisses. For a while, I had only told him goodnight with a hug and a kiss, unable to bear a routine that was missing a key element. Joe was the one who had always read to Cody. Once I got used to being the storyteller—and, in my opinion, failing at doing much more than reading—my mom let me help with dinner, clean the house, and go with her to drop Cody off at daycare. She didn't require me to do many of these things alone—or even well, for that matter. Instead, she allowed me to find a routine by working together with her, as a team.

As my mom encouraged me to take on more responsibilities, I began to embrace them. There was a strange peace in our new routine, in knowing our plans and what would happen next. I had started to accept that we don't have a lot of control in our lives, but we *can* control the tasks we do and when we do them. Planning a routine let me feel some control, even though certain circumstances would interrupt that routine occasionally. I hadn't felt in control of my life since I had kneeled next to Joe the night he had died. Now my routine with my mom reminded me that, even though I couldn't control everything in my life, I could still control some things. I could control myself.

My mom never bossed me around or told me what to do. She was a calm, regular presence, taking care of my shell and my kids and encouraging me to do whatever I could. She would push just a little, like a physical therapist working to strengthen a patient's body. She never complained about anything either—not to me, at least. She never even said anything about the fact that I kept the house's thermostat around seventy-five degrees because I was still in shock, freezing without Joe's warmth.

Sometimes she mentioned that she would need to go back to work at some point. However, she never threatened me with an end date. It would have been so easy for her to push me, to tell me she couldn't stay forever and I needed to get myself together. But she didn't. She never pried or forced anything. Instead, she was simply there, helping with whatever she could and giving me time alone when I wanted it. Today, I can't imagine what she must have gone through, especially on those nights when she must have heard me crying behind closed doors or in the shower. I was blessed with a mom who did the best she could for me, even though she may have wished I had talked to her more often. That was exactly what I needed.

With my mom's support, I continued to piece my soul back together. Kintsugi is the Japanese art of repairing broken pieces of pottery. Unlike other repair methods that hide the break and blend in the repair, kintsugi highlights the areas of breakage using powdered gold, silver, and platinum. In this way, it allows the history, the story of the piece, to be displayed. I had first heard about kintsugi when I was in middle school, from an art teacher who talked about art from different cultures. She showed us pictures of kintsugi. One vase in particular had shining veins of metal that spread across its blue surface. It looked like it had been made that way. At the time, I thought it was a neat, resourceful idea. But I didn't realize it would come back to me later, as I was rebuilding my soul after Joe's death. Loving and losing Joe was part of my story now; and as horrible as the end of our fairy tale was, it was part of the life I was still creating. I didn't want to hide it or pretend it hadn't happened. I imagined the platinum weaving through my soul as, piece by piece, I embraced my grief and cautiously stepped back into the world.

What choice did I have, anyway? People often told me how strong I was and that they didn't know how I could live with such grief. My response was always "thank you," but internally I'd scream, "*What choice do I have?*"

At that point, I thought strength was the opposite of weakness. But it's not. Strength is going on in spite of weakness, grief, fear, and brokenness. I didn't know I was strong because I was defining strength in the wrong way. Moving forward after trauma is a choice, and making that choice requires an unknown strength defined not by one's lack of weakness, but by one's decision not to give up.

So, without knowing it, I made the only choice I had: to move forward, pick up the boulder of grief I'd forever shoulder, and build myself stronger than I had been before, infused with platinum. And I knew it was right. Even though I'd lie in bed, succumbing to the fatigue of grief and wishing I could join Joe, or ask God why I wasn't the one He had taken, I had a responsibility to Joe, our sons, and—most importantly—myself. Joe may have been dead, but his opinion still mattered to me, and he had left an imprint on my soul. He wouldn't have wanted me to wallow in grief and let its darkness fill me with sadness and bitterness. I wanted to make him proud. So, piece by tiny fractured piece, I glued myself back together and slowly began my new life.

For a few fleeting movements, I began to feel like myself. I wasn't the Autumn I had known before; that woman was in a grave with my thirty-year-old husband. Instead, I was the Autumn I needed to become, a woman who shared a number of similarities with the previous version of herself. I had the same family, pets, cars, house, and job as before. But in many other ways, I was completely different.

In addition, I finally felt for people. Yes, I had cared in the past when I heard a sad story, but only on a superficial level. I hadn't known, down in my soul, what those sad stories really meant to the people involved. So I'd react like a news reporter, easily switching from talking about cute puppies to murder and then to weather. But now I could relate in a way that only those who have suffered the unthinkable truly can. I felt their pain and suffering when I heard about their cancer diagnosis or their loss of a child or spouse, and I'd cry more easily than I had before.

On the flip side, I no longer cared about listening to people complain about their rough days, how annoying their husbands were, or how much it sucked when their spouse was out of town for a few days. Pettiness became something I just couldn't tolerate, along with whining and complaining. I had no patience for it, because what did it matter? How does a rough day compare to someone dying? It doesn't get much rougher than that. On my better days, I would hold my tongue and walk away. But on my worse days, I'd say something like, "At least your husband is still alive," then walk away. This wasn't a great way to maintain relationships. Not everyone understood how I felt, and those people slowly drifted away from me. But the people who did understand didn't hold it against me.

Seven weeks after Joe died, I was going to pick up Cody from daycare when I asked myself, "What am I doing?" As I sped along the highway into town, I noticed the sky was a soft blue, the sun was shining on the grass, and trees were newly coming to life after a long winter; and I realized how much I liked having my personal space. Rather than sitting in the living room chair, oblivious to everything, I was beginning to notice what was going on around me. And despite Joe's absence, I was starting to feel claustrophobic in my house.

Until that point, I hadn't realized that having my mom at home was limiting my ability to have my own space. I had always prided myself on being self-sufficient, but I hadn't been doing that. That morning, for the first time since Joe had died, I realized I could take care of myself—and I needed my own space. I needed that room to sit with everything that had happened and create my own plan forward. My mom had been taking care of everything, but I was the only one who could decide what to do with my life. I was no longer scared to be in a space that was void of Joe. It would be hard, and I knew I'd cry and feel alone and hopeless. But I needed that space; I had always needed it. At family events, I'd often migrate to a quieter room away from the crowds or sit on the edge of the activity. Just like at that first Christmas with Joe, where I had found him sitting quietly with other members of my family, I needed to find a place where I could just be, with no one rushing around me.

So I told my mom it was time for her to go home. I hesitated doing so, since I didn't want her to think I didn't appreciate her support. When I finally spat it out, she looked at me not with sadness (which was what I was expecting), but with pride and happiness that I was healing. I don't remember what she said, but

I knew from her expression that she agreed it was time to go. She knew I was ready and that I would be OK.

Looking back on that moment, I wonder how much my mom helped remind me of who I was and how much she orchestrated my reconstruction. My parents had raised me to be independent, to be comfortable with myself in my own space. They had raised me to be strong yet flexible, to work hard but still play and have fun, to get up after falling down. Now it was time for me to get up. Losing Joe had knocked me down, but it was time for me to stand up again, remember how I wanted to live, and start believing in myself more. I didn't want to live in a world without Joe, but I didn't have a choice. I needed to choose how I was going to live without him and in the best way possible. It was what Joe would have wanted—and what I wanted. That was what I chose when I told myself it was time for my mom to go home: to stand up, trust myself, and live life, not just survive it.

I knew I'd have to make that choice again, every time life would knock me down, but that was OK. I was standing up now. Maybe it wasn't just a coincidence that the day I decided it was time for my mom to go home coincided with when she needed to return to work. Maybe she had orchestrated it perfectly, slowly helping me to my feet without rushing me. Or maybe God had planned it that way, or it was just a coincidence. Regardless, it was time to move forward using my love for Joe. That way, I could become the kind, understanding, patient person I wanted to be. I could help others and make sure they knew how much I loved them. I didn't want to be bitter and negative about my life. I had loved Joe, and he had loved me. The years we spent together, that love, transcended the loss. I would make my life transcend that loss too.

10

W
HEN I WENT BACK TO work, I found myself in a supportive environment. No one mentioned the fact that I wore my moccasin slippers to work for weeks. (While I was managing to come to work, the thought of putting on shoes was exhausting once I got the boys and myself ready.) I didn't want to be given special treatment, but I appreciated that I wasn't pushed to do more than I was capable of.

Because I was working again and my mom had gone home, I created a new routine for my family. In the morning, I'd get out of bed, prepare myself and my sons for the day ahead, drop them off at daycare, and go to work. Later, I'd pick the boys up, feed them dinner, put them to bed, do chores around the house, and finally relax for the night.

Before Joe had died, I'd sit and read for hours, watch TV, or simply be. I didn't mind alone time or silence then. But afterward, doing those activities was very difficult. I couldn't focus on anything for long. I did read some books about grief, though, and found some hope and guidance in Martha Whitmore Hickman's *Healing After Loss: Daily Meditations for Working Through Grief* and Carole Brody Fleet and Syd Harriet's *Widows Wear Stilettos: A Practical and Emotional Guide for the Young Widow*. But those books only held my attention for so long. And when I would watch TV, I'd play a mindless game on my phone to distract myself from negative thoughts such as, "My life isn't supposed to be this way." Sitting and just happily being by myself was no longer possible.

When I was by myself, I'd think about how alone I was, how this shouldn't have happened, how the future I had imagined was no longer possible. A completely healthy thirty-year-old man with a wife, two kids, a house, and plans and dreams doesn't just die. But Joe did.

Sometimes I'd have panic attacks. My heart would feel like it was about to explode, and I wouldn't be able to breathe. I would try to picture my future, but I saw loss, sadness, and grief for the rest of my life. I knew I'd carry my grief forever, because I would forever love Joe. "Always and forever" was what we had told each other.

Other times, I'd think back on the night Joe died and the hundreds of nights before then, searching for signs that something was wrong—and all the reasons this was my fault. I would wonder if I should have made him go to the doctor a few weeks earlier, when he had a case of mild heartburn, even though it was gone an hour later after he took an antacid. Or if I should have asked him not to go running that night, that it was too late and he needed to be at home. Would that have saved him? Logic told me it wasn't my fault, but emotionally I felt I should have done more.

Eventually I did everything I could not to sit with myself. To avoid thinking, I'd occupy my mind as much as possible. The more I could do at once, the more I could numb myself to those thoughts. Music became my favorite distraction. I would sit and listen to Micky and the Motorcars, Reckless Kelly, Randy Rogers Band, American Aquarium, or any other band that seemed to feel their music, and I'd think about the people in each song instead of my own life. I would feel their pain and sadness, their happiness and love; and I'd find ways to relate to them. It helped me drown out my emotions with theirs while giving me a small outlet for my own. Music fed my soul in a way nothing else would.

Around that time, I found out that Micky and the Motorcars, one of my favorite music groups, was playing in Boise, Idaho, on April 2. Even though I was functioning more than I had been, I knew my parents would worry if I embarked on a six-hour round-trip drive to a concert at a bar by myself. So I messaged two other people who liked the same music: a girl I'd been friends with for years, and Kyle, the acquaintance from work who had visited me after Joe died. My friend and Kyle knew each other because they had gone to school together, and I felt they could entertain each other and leave me alone so I could just be with the music. I had always been a little awkward when interacting with others, and now putting effort into a social event seemed like more than I could handle.

Luckily, they both agreed to go. Kyle got us good tickets for the show; we'd be upstairs, where we could sit at a table and look down on the stage instead of stand in the crush of people below. But on the night of the concert, just as we were getting ready to leave town, my friend got a call from Kyle. His mom was having a sudden medical procedure in Bend. Kyle's dad had passed away seven years earlier, so it was important that Kyle be there with his mom. He dropped off the tickets with us and quickly left for the two-hour drive to Bend.

Suddenly I saw Kyle a little differently. I looked back on how he had behaved toward me after Joe had died. He had brought practical items for the house, helped with chores I couldn't do myself, and used just a few words to show me empathy without pity. He had willingly looked me in the eyes and told me he was sorry, but he hadn't offered "advice" on how to get over the loss. Kyle didn't hide from my grief because he had experienced his own. He had gone into the darkness after losing his father, survived, and learned to be a light for others, including me.

When Kyle told us why he couldn't make the concert, I imagined his fear of losing his mom and his need to be there with her. In the past, I probably would have thought about it for a moment, then moved on to enjoy the concert. Now, however, I wanted to help. I knew I couldn't fix it, but I wanted to do something. It didn't matter that I barely knew Kyle. What I did know was he had been willing to help me—a complete stranger—when I was grieving, and I wanted to help him with this.

My friend gave me Kyle's phone number, and I sent him a text, saying my parents lived in Bend and he could crash at their house or borrow their camper if he needed a place to stay. He turned it down, but I hoped he realized someone was concerned and wanted to be there for him.

A few days later, after thinking about someone else's problems instead of my own, I finally sent Kyle another text: "Hey, how's your mom doing?" It felt good to talk to someone and focus on them instead of myself.

He responded, "She's doing good. No complications or anything. How was the concert?"

I was happy to hear his mom was doing well, but I also liked that Kyle just asked about my weekend. Not how I was doing or if I were OK, but a simple "How was your weekend?" It was a question that millions of people were asked each day. But for me, as I was still figuring out my new life, it was the "normal" question I needed, one that led to a simple and unrestrained conversation.

That conversation opened a door to a friendship I hadn't known I needed. On that first day, we sent six messages. The next day, we sent eleven, then twenty, then forty-eight. Each day we built on what we knew about each other. Through those texts,

Kyle quickly became my person, though not in a romantic sense. I still loved Joe, and I had learned I would always grieve for him.

Joe had been the one person in the world who had known everything about me. I had shared all my secrets with him. He would look at me and be able to tell how I was feeling. And when the words I'd use to explain myself were inadequate, he would understand what I meant. Joe may have been my soul mate, but he was gone. I had an opening for someone new. Someone who knew loss and trauma, someone who I could talk to about them and who would understand without judging me.

Don't get me wrong—I was surrounded by lots of amazing people who tried to understand. But most of them didn't have the same experience with grief that I had, and I didn't want them to be able to relate to it. So I turned to Kyle. We talked about everything, from our losses, our health, and the stupid things people say to you when you're grieving to books, music, TV, and movies. We also talked about family, my sons, and Joe.

I told Kyle how people who had treated me like a competent, independent, functioning adult were suddenly treating me like a confused, helpless teenager who was unable to do anything on her own. He quickly, and gently, reminded me that they didn't have a clue about navigating around my grief (which was very different than their own) or dealing with this new version of me. It was a learning curve for all of us. He also reminded me that, while it was OK to be frustrated with people and to tell them so, it would help everyone if I tried to be a little more patient, especially with family and friends.

We talked about fear too. No one really associates fear with grief—until you've been through it, that is. You become afraid of losing the people you love. You recognize you're no longer in control, or that you never really were from the start. You become fearful of life, the future, injury, loss, and death. And that fear is always there, a black shadow lurking everywhere. It reminds us that our worlds can change in an instant and love may not be enough to save anyone.

And, not surprisingly, we talked about Joe a lot. I learned that Kyle and Joe had been friends, and Kyle shared with me some of their conversations that I hadn't been aware of. All three of us had worked for the same employer; and because of that, Kyle had known and respected Joe. Their conversations had focused mostly on hunting, something they had both loved.

Our conversation about Joe wasn't forced. Kyle seemed to realize that others often avoided mentioning Joe and that I needed more than anything to talk about it. Maybe people didn't want to remind me Joe had died, or it hurt too much for them to mention his name. Still, Joe wasn't talked about enough. There were so many good memories of him, so many stories about him that I loved to hear or hadn't heard yet. I wanted to hear his name spoken out loud. It was the best way to acknowledge his loss without letting the ending ruin the rest of his wonderful story and the legacy he had left behind.

I would lie in bed with the TV on, forgetting the pointless smartphone games as I waited raptly for Kyle's next message about his conversations with Joe. I would imagine Joe drooling as Kyle talked about working in Utah and hunting opportunities for mule deer there, and then I'd smile. Joe's conversations with Kyle were likely why Joe, before his death, had suddenly started talking and dreaming about hunting in Utah one day.

Kyle didn't try to fix me or make me smile. He was just there for me, in a way no one else had been. I could talk to him anytime. He told me he put his phone on silent when he went to sleep so I could message him whenever I wanted, even at three o'clock when the darkness seemed overwhelming. At first I thought he didn't sleep much, and there was no reason we shouldn't talk if he were awake. But I needed to have someone to talk to, someone to reach out to at any time. So I chose to believe him, though he later told me he stopped silencing his phone the night we started talking.

II

WHEN JOE DIED, I WANTED to know why. I wanted to try to explain or rationalize it. Eventually I learned it doesn't make a difference. Knowing why wouldn't change things. Joe was dead regardless. Sometimes I still wish I knew because I want to protect my kids, but it doesn't matter. The *why* doesn't bring Joe back. In instances like this, no answers you find in this world will make you feel better. You can accept the loss and move forward, but it will never be OK. And because it will never be OK, the *why* doesn't matter as much. It will never be OK that the one you loved died, and answers to the questions that seemed so important at first no longer matter. Sometimes when I talk about Joe, I don't even remember to say what happened, because it doesn't matter. What matters now is what happens in the future, and that's something I have some control over.

Grief does weird things to you. For me, it was strange that Joe's death affected me in other ways besides the grief and the pain of loss. My self-confidence was broken. Maybe it was because I had tied myself and who I was to Joe. But when I tried to look to the future, I felt I was damaged goods. Early on, I wanted to eventually find somebody else to love. Joe had given me that gift. But I assumed this would be years down the road, once I figured out how to let someone new into my heart while it still loved Joe. Just thinking about dating gave me doubts. Dating is hard at any age; I couldn't imagine it being easier during my thirties. Plus, I didn't know how to approach it. How could I date and raise my kids right? How would I even find someone to date? And behind those thoughts lay my real concerns. How could I love two men? Why would anybody want to date me? It was hard for me to see my own value.

How grief can rob you of your confidence is something I'll probably never know. Maybe it's the lack of control you suddenly feel, or the fear that you can't always change things no matter what you do. But overnight, I went from a confident, happy, productive, educated, strong mom and wife who felt loved and valued by someone other than her family to a woman who had lost her soul mate and one true love. And while I wasn't even considering dating or falling in love at that time, I couldn't help but feel like it would never happen. Perhaps I felt that way because I saw myself as broken. My life and soul, everything I was, had shattered the night Joe died, and I hadn't fully put myself back together yet. I had no idea where I fit into the world or how I'd get through this. Nor did I understand why anyone would want to be around me other than my family, who were stuck with me.

But when I talked to Kyle, I felt like I still had value. I could be a friend to someone, at the very least.

At that point, no one knew Kyle and I were talking. We weren't hiding it; rather, it was only happening in our little world. He gave me the support I needed, in the way I needed it. Through his messages, Kyle took care of me the way a longtime friend, close sibling, or someone who had experienced trauma would. He was my light in the darkness when I couldn't find my own. He gave me hope. When I had a rough day, he would gently remind me it would suck for a long, long time, and it would still be sad after that, but eventually the memories would put a smile on my face. He told me I'd be able to think about Joe and how he would smile and laugh at certain things. He let me know it was OK to smile and cry, to be happy and sad. He also told me one day I'd understand the full meaning of the word *bittersweet* but couldn't rush it. I wanted to rush it so badly, though. But in Kyle's words, I saw a tiny glimmer. I would always miss and love Joe, but maybe one day I'd be happy again.

Maybe my life wasn't really over at age thirty-one. Maybe I could do more than survive.

A few days after Kyle and I started talking, someone suggested that I be careful when talking with men, as I wouldn't want them or their wives or girlfriends to think I was hitting on them or leading them on. I was shocked by that advice. I would never hit on a guy in a relationship. In fact, I had barely hit on any guys—even single ones—when I was younger. Why would grief make me start now? And who felt they had a right to talk to me about stuff like that when I was the only widow I knew? Still, I didn't want to do anything that would reflect badly on Joe. The line between what Joe would want me to do and what others would see was often blurred. While Joe would have trusted me and my judgment, others knew me only superficially and would judge me based on what they saw and not who I was.

I shared the comment with Kyle, just to be sure he didn't feel like I was leading him on. He assured me it wasn't an issue. We were having friendly conversations, and I needed a friend. That was it. I was Joe's wife, and I always would be.

The first time Kyle came to the house after Joe's funeral, he helped me watch a TV show. Joe and I had recorded a miniseries called *Texas* and planned to watch it together. I still wanted to watch it, but seeing it there in our DVR was like one more loose string waving in the wind and hitting me in the face, constantly reminding me of things I had planned with Joe. And though I felt a need to watch it for Joe's sake, I didn't want to do it by myself. I wasn't sure what emotions I'd face, and I didn't want to face them alone.

When Kyle got there, he settled into the couch while I sat in Joe's recliner, and we started talking. I had the TV on and ready to play the show, but we never even got to it. We sat on opposite sides of the room and talked for hours. It was the first real conversation I'd had, with no restraints, since Joe had died. So many of my conversations with other people had been filled with awkwardness. They didn't know what to say to me or were nervous they would say something that would bring fresh tears to my eyes, and I'd respond with my own nervousness over saying something they wouldn't understand or that would evoke a look of pity from them. None of that awkwardness existed between me and Kyle, though.

There was comfort in talking to Kyle in person, in being able to see and hear him and know I could be myself. I could let my guard down and be sad without being judged or pitied. Even though it was dark outside, it felt like the sun had come out, as if lights were shining down on us more brightly and things were clearer. Yes, the grief was still there. I often felt like the darkness surrounded me, blurring the edges of my vision and making me feel like sadness could overwhelm me at any point. But as Kyle and I talked, that darkness and threat of overwhelming sadness seemed further away. It was like he had brought within him a lamp that pushed the darkness away and created a circle of light and warmth I had been missing. I basked in that glow, and my soul began to stretch and grow; and I knew that maybe there was still a life out there for me, and maybe it wouldn't be that bad.

Later, I learned about a music festival in June that I wanted to go to in Filer, Idaho. Naturally, Kyle was the first person I asked and the only person I could convince to go with me. So we packed up Joe's truck and camper and started the five-hour drive. Kyle understood me, and I felt I understood him. We could have great conversation or companionable silence. While no man likes to see a woman cry, I knew Kyle would understand when I did (which was inevitable) and would be fine with it. He would be fine with me and whatever emotions I would throw at him.

I was lucky he would do that for me, because over that weekend I threw it all at Kyle. It started in Boise, where we stopped and watched a movie, but I wound up vomiting in the bathroom and sleeping next to a bowl. I felt better in the morning, though, and we made it to the music festival.

We had a great weekend, but for the first time I was disappointed that Kyle stayed strictly in the friend zone. I would set our chairs next to each other, only to have Kyle move them a few inches apart so our arms wouldn't touch. In the evenings, he would give me time to get changed and situated in my sleeping bag on the queen bed before coming into the camper and settling into his own sleeping bag on the smaller bed. If there was any flirting, it was on my end; I was just trying to get a reaction out of him. Joe had only been dead a few months, and I wasn't looking for a relationship. But I noticed a new kind of loneliness in my life. There was room for someone else, even if I didn't know what I wanted from them. I wasn't sure what I wanted from Kyle that weekend. Was it just attention? To feel attractive and desirable? A boost of confidence? Or was I looking for more? Was it just Kyle? Or was it anyone? Those feelings surprised me.

Over the next few weeks, I decided it was just Kyle. Somewhere along the way, he became not just my person in grief, but also my best friend. He made me happy in a way I hadn't thought possible. He let me grieve how I needed, figuratively holding my hand through it all. He made me feel confident and good about myself. He made me truly smile. Why shouldn't we date?

It took me a while to be sure I wasn't using Kyle to fill this glaring hole in my life. But there was no replacing Joe. He was one of a kind, and any "replacement" for him would be a cheap replica that wouldn't provide any satisfaction or real happiness. What I felt when I was with Kyle was real, though. The smiles and laughs came willingly. While Joe couldn't be replaced, what I found instead was an opening for a best friend: someone who I could talk to, someone who would know and keep all my secrets and like me anyway. Looking for someone to fill those shoes was my way of moving forward and trying to live without Joe. The thought of loving someone else was thrilling but scary. What if I lost Kyle too? What if he got sick and died? Or were in an accident? I thought of a million what-ifs, but eventually I settled on the simple truth: loving Joe was worth every second of pain I had felt since he had died. I didn't think loving Kyle would be any less worthwhile.

What really made a difference to me was that I felt I had Joe's permission. That made it easier to take the risk, but I was still worried. I was worried that people would think that I didn't love Joe enough, I had gotten over the loss too quickly, or Kyle was taking advantage of me. None of these things were true, of course. But I couldn't control what people thought, and I knew what they would think would matter to me.

Still, one night in early July, Kyle and I were sitting in his living room (a rare occasion when someone else was watching my boys for a few hours) when I said, "I think we should date." I simply flung the topic out there, with no real introduction.

Kyle looked at me, his expression a mixture of surprise and happiness. He leaned forward and rested his arms on his knees.

"I don't know if you are ready for that. For a relationship. I don't want to take advantage of you. You're still grieving."

"Yeah, so?" I replied. "You've done nothing but help me with my grief. You've given me permission to cry or laugh or scream. Plus, you told me I'll never really stop grieving. If that's true, then I'll never be ready to date." The satisfaction of using his own words to counter his argument brought a small smile to my face.

"People will talk," Kyle said. "We're lucky people at work haven't already seen your car parked in my driveway and started talking. Plus, what about Joe's family? What will they think?" He frowned as he sat back in his chair.

"People haven't noticed because we haven't been flaunting it or hiding it," I pointed out. "That wouldn't have to change if we started dating. I think I'm ready to date you. Probably not anyone else, but you've become my best friend in this. I don't want to let what other people think keep me from something amazing." My heart was beating fast in my chest as I anxiously waited for his answer.

"Are you sure?" he asked quietly.

"Yes, I'm sure," I said, smiling as a smile of his own lit up Kyle's face.

At some point, Kyle no longer saw me as just Joe's wife, but as a woman who would always be Joe's wife but could be more. My perception of him had changed too; I saw him as not just a co-worker or friend, but also someone I wanted to spend all my spare time with. So in the end, we decided to give it a shot. The happiness we had found in being together made the risks worthwhile.

We took things slowly and kept it quiet. We didn't hide it, but we didn't advertise it either. I also made sure we went on dates when Cody and Wade would have a babysitter or only after they were asleep. I was pretty sure I was ruining my sons' lives even without adding the man I was dating into the equation. But I still didn't want to risk them getting attached to someone I couldn't guarantee would stick around. I wanted to do right by them, but maybe I could make that happen and still do something for myself.

Don't get me wrong—I had amazing happiness with Joe. He was my soul mate, my one true love for my former life, and our memories are worth more to me than anything else. But that life had died with him. Now, my soul and all of me were different. Maybe that kind of love was possible again. I was recreating myself in the kintsugi style, and maybe the new me would find something just as wonderful, though completely different from what I'd had with Joe. If that were possible, then how could I turn my back on it? After all, wasn't loving Joe worth the loss? I wasn't trying to replace Joe, since there was no such thing. You can't recreate something— or someone—that's been lost; you can only create something new. Love is original. Joe was part of my story, and now Kyle was too.

When Kyle and I started dating, I was still wearing my wedding band and engagement ring from Joe. Sometimes I'd take my rings off. Other times, I'd wear them. Eventually I put the engagement ring in the safe. I didn't want to risk losing it in case Cody or Wade wanted to use it in the future. My wedding ring still bounced around, though. I would alternate between putting it on the proper finger or my right ring finger or leaving it on my jewelry box. I needed to wear it, but I wasn't sure how Kyle would feel. I didn't want him to think I wasn't taking our relationship seriously. It seemed silly, though. They were just rings, after all.

One day, not long after we started dating, Kyle asked, "Why did you take your rings off?" There was no judgment in his voice; just a simple, casual curiosity.

"I don't know," I said. "I just thought maybe I should." To be honest, I didn't know if I was still supposed to wear my ring.

Legally I was no longer married. Plus, in some of the Facebook groups I was part of, many people said that continuing to wear my rings would be inconsiderate to Kyle. But without my ring on my finger, I felt like something was missing, like I wasn't honoring my commitment to Joe.

Kyle, however, touched my cheek and gently tucked a strand of hair behind my ear. "You don't need to do that," he said. "Not for me. You love Joe. You always will, and you were his wife. Loving Joe, and losing him, is a part of your story. That will always be true no matter if your rings are on or off. You do what you need to do. Don't worry about me."

I slowly raised my eyes up to meet Kyle's, tears running down my face. "Thank you," was the only response I had as I started to fall in love with him.

EVEN TODAY, I CAN only imagine how difficult the situation must have been for Kyle. He was there willingly, and he was amazing. But how can you step into a relationship with a woman who still regularly cries for her husband? A woman who wakes up from nightmares where her husband has abandoned her only to remember that he's dead? A woman you would do anything for—even bring her husband back, if it were possible—just to end her suffering, even though it would increase your own?

When Kyle and I first started spending time together, I told the people I cared about, including my family and Joe's. I had become a celebrity in our small town so quickly after Joe's death, so it was only a matter of time before someone would notice Kyle's truck at my house or my car at his. It didn't matter that Joe's mom lived in a different state at that point. News would travel fast, and I didn't want her to be caught off guard.

Those conversations were easy. However, once Kyle and I began dating, I needed to have more difficult discussions with Joe's family. I told his brother first, thinking that would be the easiest one to start with. We were in my living room, and I was sitting in Joe's recliner and Joe's brother on an ottoman across the room.

"Kyle and I started dating," I blurted out. "I didn't plan on it happening. But I have feelings for him, and I want to see where they go."

Joe's brother didn't reply. He only watched me quietly.

"We're going to take it slow," I went on, avoiding his gaze for fear of what I'd see in his face. "I'll always love Joe, but I need to do this. The boys don't know anything about him, and won't unless it gets that serious."

When I finished, I clasped my hands and sat there quietly, trying not to appear anxious. I felt Joe's brother's eyes on me the whole time. When he finally spoke, his answer wasn't what I expected.

"You're my sister," he said softly and with kindness in his voice. "I want what's best for you. I'll support you no matter what. Just take care of the boys. Make sure they don't get hurt."

I looked at Joe's brother then and felt the weight of worry leave my body. The relief of having his support meant more to me than I could ever say. I had been so nervous that he would be angry, and I wouldn't have blamed him if he had reacted that way. It was strange even to me that I wanted to date while still grieving and very much in love with Joe. But no matter what Joe's brother may have felt, he still chose to be supportive, and I cried about it after he left.

Telling Joe's mom was more difficult. She had moved away from Burns after Joe finished high school and now lived seven hours away. That meant telling her on the phone rather than in person, where she would have been able to read my body language.

I paced the floor, too anxious to sit still, as I told her what I had already told Joe's brother. I also told her that I would always love Joe and I knew he would be OK with it, and that I wanted her to find out from me rather than anyone else. Joe's mom's voice was full of tears and emotion as she said OK and rushed to hang up.

Though I had tried to be gentle, I knew it had hurt her to learn her daughter-in-law was in a relationship with another man— someone who wasn't her son—just months after Joe died. Maybe she felt as though I had found a replacement for Joe already. Or maybe she worried I'd remarry and she would never see Cody and Wade again. That last bit wouldn't have happened, but I knew how easy it was to fear the worst. I would never presume to know what thoughts went through her head that evening. But when I hung up the phone, I felt like I had let her down. She would likely call her friends and Joe's over the next few days, asking them how I could do such a thing. But I was glad that she had people she felt comfortable talking to—and that at least a few of the people she and I both knew supported me. They may not have agreed with my choice to date Kyle, but their encouragement bolstered me and made me feel so much better about it.

Joe's mom, I realized, would have to process this new relation- ship and work through her grief. But for those few weeks after our conversation, it seemed like she would never forgive me, and I was hurt by her reaction. I needed her support and felt I hadn't received it. So I was surprised when she finally called and gave me her full approval and then some. She welcomed Kyle not just into my life, but also into hers, and with open arms.

Months later, Joe's mom would invite me, Kyle, and the boys to her house for a visit. One morning, I got up early while Kyle was showering and the boys were still sleeping. When I walked into the living room, Joe's mom was sitting on her couch.

"Sit down with me a minute," she said. "It's been nice seeing you and Kyle here. He's great with the boys."

"I'm glad we were able to come," I said, trying to keep myself from crying. "I know it isn't easy for you."

She looked at me for a moment. "Yes, it's hard. It's hard for all of us. I can see that Kyle loves you and the boys. And if I've learned anything in my life, I've learned that there's always room for more love."

I sat there in awe. Joe's mom's willingness to accept that Kyle and I were together, and her permission for us to love each other, was such a relief. More importantly, she understood that loving Kyle didn't diminish my love for Joe.

My love for Kyle was in fact growing, even though I still loved Joe with every ounce of my soul. But that love for Joe wasn't decreasing. If anything, it increased in a way that happens when someone you love dies and lives only in your memories. And as my love for Kyle grew, I learned that love isn't mutually exclusive; in other words, one love doesn't replace another. They can coexist in one's heart, but they're completely different.

12

WHILE I HAD FINALLY FOUND someone I could talk to, I still hadn't found someone who understood the depth of losing a spouse. I didn't know any widows, even in my own family, since my grandparents were still alive and married. So finding a widow who was around my age and had young kids seemed impossible.

Kyle understood grief but not widowhood. He may have supported me and my feelings, but just as I couldn't fully understand Kyle's grief over losing his dad, Kyle couldn't fully grasp how I felt after losing Joe. He couldn't comprehend my irrational desire to tell my dead husband about my new boyfriend or what it was like to date one man and still feel married to another. He gave me hope when we were together, but when we weren't, it was so easy for that little light to fade out and leave me in the darkness again.

When you lose a spouse, you deal with certain things that are unique to that loss. For example, someone offered to make quilts, bears, and pillows out of Joe's clothes, so cleaning his jeans and shirts out of his closet wasn't that hard for me. I knew they would come back to us as something tangible. But what the hell do you do with someone's underwear? No matter how new Joe's were, it seemed weird to use them in quilts or give them to other people. I threw them away in the end, though it was something I struggled with.

And what about the three new deodorants Joe had just bought? That also seemed weird to give away, especially since they had been opened. But they were his, and I hated being wasteful. So I decided to use them. (Since then, I've learned I don't go through deodorant as fast as Joe did. I'm just finishing up the last of the three, five years after his passing.)

Everyone experiences grief in different ways. Your sense of grief also changes based on who you lose. I wanted to find someone who could tell me it was normal to struggle with what to do with my dead husband's underwear. I needed someone who could verify I was OK—or at least that I wasn't alone in how I was feeling, acting, and reacting in my grief.

I joined some groups for widows on Facebook. I rarely posted, but reading the stories of others like me would sometimes help. On one hand, I learned about widows who put crackers in the freezer and keys in the refrigerator, or left their car running in the driveway after coming home. These were stories I could relate to because I had done similar things so many times in the past few months. But on the other hand, these groups were full of posts by widows who were two, four, or even ten years removed from their losses and saying how they still cried every day, how they still struggled to get up in the mornings, how smiles and laughter were still rare in their lives. Those stories scared me, but also motivated me to work through my grief even more.

Though I found comfort in knowing I wasn't alone, I also feared what my future would be like. I didn't want to be in a place where I was acutely miserable for the rest of my life. I needed to find a way to enjoy life as much as possible. I wanted to travel and see things I never thought I'd see. I wanted to be comfortable in my new life, not constantly fighting grief and sadness. I wanted to laugh, live, and love. I would experience periods of hope, where I felt like I was healing and growing in my grief. But these moments would often be followed by periods of depression, where

I'd struggle to hang onto that hope. If I were going to survive this loss, I would need more help than I had found online or in books.

One evening, while searching for other groups online, I found an organization called Soaring Spirits. Their website advertised their focus on helping widowed people learn to live without the loved ones they have lost. It featured pictures of widows of all ages, smiling, laughing, and looking happy. Their motto was (and still is) Hope Matters.

Soaring Spirits seemed to offer exactly what I was looking for. So when I discovered they held a camp for widows, fittingly called Camp Widow®, I knew I needed to go.

I had always hated school and work activities that involved sharing and team building. But in this instance, I knew I needed to be in an environment that would put me in all those situations I hated but for the right reasons. For the first time in my life, I considered going to a social situation so I could help myself. I needed more than lying in bed for hours, trying to distract myself from the pain, loss, and darkness. I needed to talk to people who understood what I was going through and who I could talk to about Joe and how I lost him. I also needed people who I could talk to about Kyle, who understood my conflicting emotions and offered help or at least listened without the judgment I so feared. So in July, five months after Joe had passed, I traveled to Camp Widow® in San Diego, California.

Despite the name, Camp Widow® isn't a traditional camp. Some may argue it's more of a retreat, since it takes place at four-star hotels, like the one I attended on the San Diego Bay waterfront. Here, you're surrounded by as much physical comfort as possible. That was what I noticed when I walked into Camp Widow®. Shortly after that, I was warmly welcomed by their staff of volunteers, who were smiling, hugging, laughing, and wearing shirts labeled with sayings such as Hope Matters, Death Sucks, Long Live Love, and Widows Rock. I received my name tag and a badge that stated how long it had been since my loss. At that point, I was in the "less than six months" group. But as I looked around, I noticed men and women—including people my age—wearing similar badges that ranged to over ten years. Some people even wore multiple badges.

What stopped me in my tracks was seeing the smiles of the widowed people who were there. Their smiles were real, genuine, and truly happy, not the fake ones you wear so people can stop talking to you, pitying you, or worrying about you. How did I know those smiles were real? Because so many people were smiling and laughing while talking about their dead partners, often while crying and gathering around boxes of tissues. I felt like I was in a place where my loss would be understood.

I was still looking around when another widow walked over to me. "Welcome to the club no one wants to be a part of, but we're glad you found us," she said. "What was your partner's name?"

"Joe," I said shyly, still in shock from what I was seeing.

"My husband's name was John. He had colon cancer." We talked for a few more minutes before she said, "I'm sorry I had to meet you this way, but it was good talking with you." She left then to welcome other new campers, and I went to browse the books and other items at the store, many adorned with the same phrases I had seen on the volunteers' shirts.

As I spent the next three days attending workshops and round-tables led by widows and widowers, I discovered how freeing it was to talk to people without building a wall to protect myself and others from my grief, and without worrying about whether I'd cry or say the wrong thing. I didn't have to be in control of the conversation or situation. Instead, I could simply be. At Camp Widow®, everything was OK. For the first time since Joe had died, I could be real and open. People didn't look at me with pity or sadness, or see me as a victim. Rather, they looked at me with understanding and compassion and saw me as a survivor. I made connections and new friends. Listening to their stories, which were similar yet different from mine, and seeing what people were doing in the years after losing their spouse was inspiring. These stories were so much better than those I had read on Facebook. They were full of life and happiness despite what each widowed person had been through, not full of bitterness and sadness because of it. I allowed my hope to grow that weekend and felt a change deep in my soul in a place even Kyle hadn't touched.

I was still rebuilding myself in my new life, gluing the pieces back together slowly. But now I knew I could find happiness even in the midst of grief; and like kintsugi, I could be beautiful in my damage. The glue my soul needed was hope; and as more pieces settled into place, I imagined the filled cracks glowing like sun reflecting on water. I felt sunlight on my soul in the same way I had felt it warm my skin on the beach at Shore Acres. I believed I could rekindle my own light so it could shine even when I was in the darkness. And I hoped that, one day, I could do what the people at Camp Widow® did for me and be a small light for others who found themselves trapped in the darkness.

Camp Widow® changed my life. Even today, words fall short when I try to explain what that event did for me. I no longer wanted to run away. I had finally found friends who understood what it's like to lose a partner and your future together. And like me, these friends were carrying their kids through grief. They didn't judge me, my grief, or my choices, even when those choices may have been questionable. They also didn't judge me about Kyle. Some of them understood and wanted to meet someone new for themselves. Others didn't want to date ever again. None of us judged each other, though, because none of that mattered. We were all doing what we needed to do to survive. How can you judge anyone else for doing the same?

That's what most people who haven't lost a spouse don't understand: it's about survival. Some widows and widowers can't comprehend how to live without their partner and don't see it as an option. Maybe that explains why suicide rates are higher among widowed people compared to the general population. But even without suicidal thoughts, you still have to survive emotionally. You can physically survive and do what you need to do, but that doesn't mean you won't wall yourself off to protect yourself from the pain that comes with grief. At Camp Widow®, we talked about these struggles. People shared their experiences and their battles with life and death so they could help others. They demonstrated that depression and mental health need to be treated, and provided a variety of resources to anyone who needed them.

Once I went home, I knew I'd continue to struggle. Some of the talks at Camp Widow® explained that when we'd leave this bubble of hope and support, we'd likely experience "camp crash," where we might feel the other extreme. In that way, Camp Widow® didn't fix my grief or make life less complicated. I still experienced fear, sadness, and anger afterward; and the pain would take my breath away and press on my chest. But it wasn't the same as before. After Camp Widow®, even when the darkness felt suffocating, I believed I'd be able to shoulder the grief and find happiness again. I knew I could make a light in the darkness and other people were out there who really understood because they had survived and were now holding out a light and a hand to me. Even in the darkness, I wasn't alone. I just had to take the right steps and grab onto the support that was offered to me.

13

THROUGHOUT THE SUMMER, MY RELATIONSHIP with Kyle grew slowly. We were in no hurry. We just knew we had feelings for each other beyond friendship; and when we decided to date, we decided not to ignore or squash those feelings.

Dating had always been a struggle for me; I hadn't had a lot of experience with it. And when you added grief and a dead husband into the mix, it was brand new territory emotionally speaking. I was happy to be with Kyle, but I was still sad that I wasn't with Joe. I was angry that God had taken Joe from me, but I felt blessed that God had brought Kyle and me together. And I'd feel bitter at weddings, even though I would sincerely hope for the best for the bride and groom. I just wanted nothing more than to know if my husband would approve of my boyfriend, even though it wasn't possible to know that.

Late that summer, my parents invited Kyle to a lakeside camping trip for the family. It was the first time my sons would be around Kyle, so to avoid confusing them, Kyle and I agreed that he would go as a friend of mine and sleep in a tent outside our camper. Yet it still gave Kyle an opportunity to meet my parents, see where I came from, and get to know Cody and Wade better.

As the boys spent more time with Kyle, they began to build a relationship with him, not as a father figure but as a friend. I wanted to keep Cody and Wade from getting hurt in case things didn't work out between me and Kyle. I figured Kyle could continue to be a friend even if that happened, and he agreed to continue that role no matter what. I wasn't willing to have my sons bond with a man who might disappear from their life. They had already dealt with enough loss. Nevertheless, watching Kyle play with them on the beach and at the camp and build that bond made me feel lucky that I had a man who would put them first. It was a relief to see them laughing and having fun together. I needed the boys' approval of Kyle, even though Cody and Wade were both so young; and this was the first time I saw just that.

In September, on what would have been my sixth wedding anniversary with Joe, I went back to Bandon and Shore Acres, this time with Kyle. He had been so involved in my grief and heard all about my last trip there, and I wanted to share it with him. I also realized that the anniversary itself might be hard for me, and I wanted Kyle's support close by. Plus, I wanted to do something to honor Joe by going somewhere we had visited and built memories together and share them with someone else.

It sounds weird, doesn't it? To honor your dead husband with your new boyfriend? But that's what Kyle and I did. On September 5, the night of the anniversary, Kyle took me out for a nice dinner. He gave me an anniversary card, and we spent the evening talking about Joe. I shared stories and memories, laughed, and cried, all while having the quiet and strong support of a man who cared for me. Despite how unusual it was, it was just what I needed.

During that trip, I was able to breathe easier and with fewer tears. When I had visited Shore Acres before, my emotions had been raging within me, and I had seen and felt them in the landscape as I wandered around. This time, as I walked with Kyle, I felt calmer and more relaxed, with a quiet acceptance of what had happened in my life. I had a better understanding of what I could and couldn't control.

Then, a few days after we got home, life—or, more accurately, death—happened again.

ON SEPTEMBER 8, TWO days after Kyle and I returned home from the coast, we were playing with Cody and Wade when my mom called. She told me my cousin Brittany was in the hospital. At that point, I wasn't told what had happened, and no one knew what was going on. They thought it would be OK, so I stayed in Burns and thought about Brittany.

Brittany was the perfect example of quiet strength. While she was attending college in Ohio, she struggled with depression. I never talked to her about it, preferring to sit with her and relax, play cards, talk about horses, and enjoy her company. We didn't see each other often during that period, except for holidays and the occasional trip together. But when I did see her, she was the same Brittany I loved and one of my favorite people. Yet despite the fact that I knew she was struggling, I didn't understand why, which made it easier to ignore.

Before Joe had died, Brittany and I drove with our moms and sisters to Minnesota. To get some personal space, which we both valued, we would ride in the camper as the other four women rode in the truck. We were lying on the camper bed and talking, just as we'd done before on family trips. Suddenly Brittany stopped, looked at me, and told me how much she admired me. There's nothing quite like hearing from your role model that they consider you to be one of theirs.

After Joe died, Brittany had taken me into Cody's room for some privacy. She told me that she knew nothing she said would make things better, but she wanted me to know she was proud of me and always would be. She was proud of the woman, wife, and mother I had become, and she knew that somehow I would get through this. She didn't try to fix me or tell me it would be all right. Instead, she spoke from her heart, and it was perfect.

Now, while Brittany was in the hospital and I was in Burns, I worried her depression was the reason she was in the hospital. I feared she had tried to commit suicide—not because I thought she would do it, but because she was a healthy thirty-four-year-old woman and nothing else made sense. Plus, I had learned through Camp Widow® and other experiences that suicide often occurs in unexpected places. I didn't know what to think, but despite the fact that my husband had suddenly died a few months before, I wanted to believe that healthy people in their thirties didn't experience sudden and random medical issues.

I worried I had missed the signs, that I had ignored opportunities to help Brittany and missed my chance to talk to her honestly and from the heart, just as she had talked to me. Later, however, I learned that as Brittany had continued to battle depression in her adult life, she had also been experiencing what seemed to be minor health problems.

The next morning, my mom called me while I was at work. Brittany's heart was failing, and one of her lungs had collapsed. As a result, she was being transferred to Oregon Health and Science University (OHSU) in Portland. My mom told me then that Brittany had recently had headaches and periods of increased heart rate and sweating. She had gone to see a doctor, who recommended antidepressants, but her hypertensive episodes had continued. When my aunt took Brittany back to the doctor, Brittany had an episode where her blood pressure rose so high that the doctor immediately admitted her to the emergency room, where she was placed in a medically induced coma so her condition could be stabilized.

After that call, I sat at my desk for a few minutes before deciding what to do next. Brittany was a horse trainer and had a barn at my aunt and uncle's small ranch in Springfield. Her parents and her sister, as well as my parents and my sister, were heading to Portland to be with her. So I decided I needed to be at the ranch, taking care of Brittany's beloved horses and her yellow lab, Tyson.

Since I didn't know what would happen or how long I'd be there, I asked Kyle to come with me. I didn't want to be alone regardless of how things played out, and I knew I could use his presence, support, and help with Cody and Wade, especially if I went to visit Brittany in the hospital. All four of us drove the five hours to my aunt and uncle's ranch, nestled between lush green hills in the Willamette Valley. When we arrived, we fed the animals and did chores around the house. It was nice to do something instead of just sitting around, waiting for news. But soon afterward, that was all we could do: sit, wait, and pray the doctors would find the problem and Brittany would get better. That was the hardest part. You have no control in such situations. Everything was in someone else's hands. So we waited, imagining the worst while praying for the best.

Through text messages with my sister, I learned Brittany had stabilized once she reached OHSU. More importantly, the doctors had a lead on a cause: a mass on Brittany's adrenal gland that could have been a pheochromocytoma, which they could remove and treat. So she had been put on dialysis to clear her kidneys, and her heart had begun to function on its own. She also had been taken off the medications that had kept her sedated, and everyone was now waiting for her to wake up.

That evening, my sister called to tell us the good news. Things were improving, Brittany's body was functioning better, and the family was still waiting for her to wake up. I made plans before going to bed to visit Brittany in Portland the next day and convince her to come to Burns once she recovered to help me pick out the perfect horse.

Around two o'clock, my phone rang again. Having lost Joe, I realized people didn't call in the middle of the night to share good news. And before I answered the phone, I knew I wasn't ever going to have that conversation with Brittany as I had planned.

My mom was on the other end. She said Brittany's brain had stopped functioning. Brittany was still on life support, but there was no chance for recovery, and the doctors were planning to take her off it in the morning, I needed to get there right away.

I quietly cried in Kyle's arms so I wouldn't wake my sons, then got dressed and drove two hours to Portland. I spent most of that drive thanking God that the boys and I had Kyle while simultaneously cursing Him. Wasn't one sudden death in the family enough? How could this be happening? How does someone lose two of their favorite people in less than one year?

After I arrived at OHSU around five o'clock, each of us had our time to say goodbye. But what do you say? By medical standards, Brittany was already gone. My aunt believed she had seen it happen around 10:30 p.m. the night before, when Brittany had suddenly relaxed and looked more like herself. Was her spirit still there, just hanging around?

I don't remember what I told Brittany that morning. The familiar fog of shock and grief was rolling back in. Whatever I said, it probably wasn't enough. I had missed my opportunity to tell her how much she had meant to me, but I prayed she knew it somehow, better than words could have ever expressed.

When I had found Joe, his heart had already stopped. His soul was gone at that point, and yet I had tried to save him. With Brittany, though, it was different. Her body was still there, alive with the help of machines, but the cousin I loved wasn't. I saw each heartbeat as it pulsed on the monitor. It's impossible to wrap your mind around the idea that the body still functions but the brain is gone. What made it even more confusing was that my aunt, cousin, sister, and my mom chose to be close to Brittany, to hold her hands and touch her, while I stood against the wall.

When they turned off the machines, all of us surrounded Brittany, and I suddenly wished that I could have saved her. Maybe it was selfish of me, but at that moment, if there were no chance that I could save her, I didn't want to be there. While her family held her hands and touched her in farewell, I couldn't find any comfort, closure, or peace in watching her heart stop, the final sign of life ending in a straight line. I stood next to my dad, leaning back against the counter in the hospital room, trembling with grief, sadness, and the desire to be anywhere but there, watching Brittany's last moments. The only thing that kept me in that room was my uncle. Maybe he felt the same tension, that same desire to be somewhere else. If he left the room, I was going to leave too—not for Brittany, but for him. I couldn't do or say anything to make things OK. But I could give him my presence, that subtle support. My uncle stayed in the room, however, and so did I, arms wrapped around myself, fists clenched in the unfairness of it all, tears quietly running down my face. And as the sun slowly rose that morning, the world was short of yet another person I loved.

Brittany had all the symptoms of a pheochromocytoma, but the nurses and doctors hadn't been familiar enough with the condition to diagnose it sooner. Her tumor was one of the largest of its type ever seen at OHSU, and a medical paper was written about it. They estimated it had started growing about ten years earlier, when she was in college—around the same time she had started battling depression.

It still hurts that she left us so soon. But it hurts more to know she suffered for so long, unable to feel calm and confident in herself and her life, when all along a tumor had likely brought on the depression. She had been happy despite this, but she deserved more. She gave her time and attention to anyone who needed them. She let her "little buddy," as she sometimes called me, follow her around without complaint even when she was in high school, when she probably had better things to do. She constantly put others before herself; and I hope that, wherever she is now, she's finally calm and happy. Maybe she and Joe are hanging out in heaven, not saying much but enjoying each other's company nonetheless.

WHILE KYLE AND I had been taking things slowly, he was now thrown into the challenge of supporting me now that I had experienced another traumatic loss. But he seemed to know I needed him there, and he did everything I needed willingly. We stayed at my aunt and uncle's while Brittany's memorial service was arranged. The boys and I slept in a camper, with Kyle close by in his tent. He watched the boys while I helped create a slide show and a speech for the service. He helped wherever he could, sometimes walking around the ranch to see who else and how else he could help now that we were grieving for Brittany and still mourning Joe.

Though no one said so, I often felt like my family thought Joe should have been there. He hadn't just known Brittany; he had worked, laughed, and talked with her. Shouldn't Joe have been the one to take care of the boys and help out? Even though I was happy with Kyle, a part of me agreed with them. In the midst of grief, it was easy to drown in the should-have-beens. But Joe wasn't there. He shouldn't have died—and neither should have Brittany. None of this should have happened, but life doesn't care about what we think should have been.

Thinking of what should have been can understandably make people angry, sad, and bitter. And unfortunately, Kyle received some of that bitterness and anger, since some of my family members were having trouble accepting his new role in my life. It was an awful situation, but despite the tension and conflict, Kyle willingly stayed for me and my sons. It may have been selfish of me to ask him to come with us to my aunt and uncle's, but not asking probably wouldn't have kept him away. When I thanked him, he simply said, "This is what you do for people you care for."

I probably would have gotten through that time without Kyle . . . and yet I don't know how I would have done it. He was the one person who kept me grounded. With him by my side, the loss wasn't easier, but it was more bearable. And even though his presence at my aunt and uncle's home caused some tension, I loved him more for staying to support us.

14

I N FEBRUARY 2016, JUST OVER a year after Joe's death and five months after Brittany's passing, I went on a Caribbean cruise with my family to celebrate my grandparents' sixtieth wedding anniversary. Grandpa Chuck's cancer had recently gone into remission, and because some of my relatives live across the country, the cruise was a chance for my grandparents to visit with loved ones they didn't see very often. Joe and I had planned to go on the cruise together, splurging on a balcony room so we could have our own private place. But after he died, I was at a loss for what to do.

I knew I needed to go on the cruise, but I didn't want to go alone. If Brittany hadn't died, I probably would have been fine. She and I would have found quiet places where we could hang out, but that wasn't an option anymore. So I asked my sister and a friend (who had been one of Joe's best friends) to come and share a cabin with me and my cousin, Brittany's sister. I wanted to be around people who would understand if I wanted to cry or weren't having fun and would leave me alone when I needed it.

During the cruise, we walked for miles at the port cities and spent time reading, relaxing, talking about Joe, sightseeing, and just being together. I missed Kyle and my sons and thought about them often, but it was a nice break from home, where my grief and the responsibility of raising two little boys on my own were always in my face.

The cruise was more than a break, though. While it was sad to go without Joe, it was also cathartic. Going on a cruise had been on our bucket list, and I completed that item. Doing that reminded me that I could complete things on that list, or on my own bucket list, without Joe. I was capable of living my life to whatever extent I chose. My grief was still present during the cruise, of course. But by then, it was as if I were dragging my grief behind me. It was there, but out of sight.

And so my grandparents celebrated their anniversary with their six kids, a whole passel of grandkids, and a few great-grandkids who were old enough to come along. We were a family again, bound not just by blood but also by marriage and relationships. We would bicker playfully, arguing about who was Grandma's favorite and who was next to push Grandpa Chuck around in his wheelchair. It was a break for all of us, since we had come together twice in the past year to mourn two family members under the age of thirty-five.

It was a relief to celebrate the living for once, instead of honoring our dead. But that relief was short-lived.

LESS THAN A MONTH after the cruise, Grandpa Chuck's health quickly deteriorated. We had all assumed his cancer was still in remission. However, when Grandpa visited his doctor after coming home, the doctor discovered his cancer was back—and it was everywhere. Possible treatments were discussed, but it was clear they would only extend his life for a short while.

Grandpa Chuck chose not to fight it. He was ready to go, and he declined everything except comfort care. So my family once again gathered in Oregon, and my grandpa passed away quietly, surrounded by his loved ones . . . except me.

I had already visited Grandpa Chuck earlier that day. But when my family called to say they thought his time was close, I didn't go. I didn't want to. Some of my family probably questioned that choice, but I knew from experience that I wouldn't get any closure from being there and I didn't want to watch as life left someone I loved again. I needed to do what was right for me, not what was right for others. So I stayed at my aunt and uncle's house, where I acted as the hostess for others who had remained there and waited for the call.

This was my third loss in just over a year. It felt like the grief was accumulating, weighing on my shoulders—though with each loss, the grief felt different. For instance, Joe had been a part of my daily life, and his loss had shattered my soul. In many ways, I was still piecing myself back together at that time and learning to live again; I was imagining my soul like those kintsugi bowls, beautiful with the platinum glue that represented Joe. With Brittany, the future I lost was not one I shared with a spouse, but one with a relative and friend who had known me my entire life and loved me no matter what. Her death had also fragmented my soul, though the pieces were larger; and I was still putting those fragile pieces together again, this time with a golden glue to match Brittany's heart and the sunrise that had taken her to heaven.

While Grandpa Chuck's passing was sad, I learned something new from it. I would grieve for him, but my grief for him was different from my grief for Joe or Brittany. It lacked the trauma I had experienced with the other two. I felt the difference then, but only recently have I realized what that difference was: the fact that Grandpa died after a life well lived.

Many things aren't certain in life, but one of them is death. The so-called natural order of things is that you are born, grow up, get married, have a family, watch your family grow up, then die when you're old. That's how life should go, though I had learned reality doesn't always follow those rules. Just because Grandpa Chuck lived a long life doesn't mean his death was justified. However, it lacked the unfairness. I found some comfort that, while his passing was still horrible, it followed the natural order of life. It had followed a plan, whereas the losses of Joe and Brittany still didn't make sense in my head and my heart.

15

AFTER GRANDPA CHUCK PASSED AWAY, I knew I needed to keep learning how to deal with grief. It wasn't possible to get over or move on from each loss. However, I wanted to learn more about how to shoulder the weight, accept each loss, and move forward in life and love. I wanted to learn how my body and mind reacted to grief, since I was still struggling with it every day. I thought that if I could understand it more and come up with answers to my questions, maybe I could learn how to move out of the darkness without needing Kyle, or someone else, to lead me.

During that first year without Joe, sometimes I found I was doing OK. I was living on the edge of the fog that had surrounded me when Joe first died. But I was able to laugh, smile, and embrace the happiness I was feeling with Kyle and the boys. I was no longer indifferent to whether I lived or died; I wanted to live, and sometimes I could even enjoy it. Inevitably, though, I'd slip back into that acute grief, and the darkness would come. I'd feel it creeping closer, like a storm that covers the sun and its guiding light. And I didn't want to go there. I didn't want to think about the pain and loss, the sadness and hurt. I would fight it for weeks, but it would always engulf me by the end. I could never stop the storm of grief and trauma.

Each time the darkness would envelop me, I'd be exhausted. I would collapse into it, just like I had when I had first lost Joe. The confusion, shock, lethargy, pain, and fear would all come back and leave me feeling like a shell of a person, with a shattered soul. Eventually, though, I'd find my way out. Something Kyle, Cody, or Wade would say or do would provide a spark, like Wade's milestone moments of learning to walk or say "Mama." But often it was something small, like Cody giving me a bear hug and saying how strong he was, or Kyle telling me a dumb joke that I couldn't help but laugh at. Moments like these would allow me to see how blessed my life really was. They would give me something to grab on to and follow to the other side of the storm.

Each time it was over, I'd feel battered but better, as if my grief and tears had been washed with the rain that had fallen. I would escape the storm with a little bit of light that would bring back my hope and remind me that loss was shitty, horrible, and traumatic, but there was still happiness and good in the world.

And through each collapse into the darkness, Kyle would stand by me. It didn't matter if the storm lasted for a few days or a few weeks. He was always there. It must not have been easy for him, though, and he must have had doubts. Should we be dating? Would it be possible for me to truly embrace him and our relationship if I were still grieving for Joe? Did I know what I was doing? Or was I acting impulsively? I had a lot of self-doubt then too, since I still hadn't fully recovered the confidence in myself I had possessed before Joe died.

I also was afraid of being judged—and I knew it was happening. Some former friends had openly done it, telling me they thought it was too soon or Kyle wasn't the right person for me. Despite the support I was getting from the people who really mattered, I was bothered by the negative opinions of acquaintances and even strangers. So I cried . . . a lot. I wasn't much of a crier before, even boasting that I didn't have the "Grandma Ruth gene," meaning that I wouldn't tear up for everything, good or bad, like my Great-Grandma Ruth. So I hated the fact that I was crying so much then. I hated that I couldn't control the tears and they would come at any time: work, church, the grocery store, weddings, even driving. The tears always came unbidden. I didn't want people to tell me I was strong, but I was afraid of crying and of people thinking I was weak. I didn't want to be pitied or a victim, and I felt crying would make those things happen.

Just when I needed it most, my sister recommended me to a transformative coach located in Bend. My sister had started working with the coach, who had been recommended by one of her friends, shortly after Brittany had died. She felt the sessions had helped her with her grief, and she thought they might help me too. The coach asked lots of hard questions, but she also offered advice and helped my sister learn to see things from a different perspective. We hadn't been raised to believe it was normal to see a coach or therapist. In fact, I was pretty certain they were just after money. So how could I benefit from seeing one? I didn't like talking or sharing my personal business with others, and I didn't think I could find someone who would understand what I had gone through. Still, my sister said this coach had helped her deal with her own grief over Joe and Brittany as well as other areas of her life. She recommended that I try one session with the coach to see what it was like.

On my sister's word, I scheduled my first session with the transformative coach. It. Was. Horrible. When I first arrived at her office, she offered me water or tea and a comfortable chair. The surroundings were calming, and the coach was warm and welcoming. But once we started talking, it was hard. She asked questions I hadn't asked myself. For example, she asked what my intentions were with Kyle and said that if they were true and honest, then what other people thought didn't matter. I knew my intentions were good and honest, and I was comfortable with my decision. What other people thought wasn't under my control.

The coach required me to do a lot of soul-searching and wouldn't accept superficial answers or avoidance. She gently but firmly made me look inside myself in a way I hadn't done before. I cried a lot during that session. By the time I left, I felt emotionally and physically drained. But miraculously, after the insights from that session had begun to sink in, I felt much better than when I had walked into her office.

I knew I needed to keep going to these coaching sessions, at least for a while. So we arranged for more sessions every few weeks, since that was how often I could drive to Bend. Before each session, I'd be nervous, anxious, and dreading the tears I knew would come. But the draw of the feeling of peace afterward convinced me to keep going back.

During one session, I told my coach how I'd start feeling off or sad without any reason. I'd try to hide it from others and from myself. I didn't want to hurt, and I didn't think I should still hurt. After all, if I was dating Kyle, was it right for me to still be actively grieving for Joe? I told her how I questioned my own feelings, especially when other people made it clear they were questioning them as well. I also told her how I wanted to show a strong front, that I was a survivor and not a victim who was powerless over her emotions; and yet how I wanted to scream about how it wasn't fair and to tell God how much His plan sucked and how much I hated Him. And finally, I told her how I'd fight the storm and the darkness, sometimes for weeks, until I couldn't anymore; and how I'd later curl up in a ball, usually at night when I was alone in my bed, and pull the covers over my head to shut out the world. I made it clear that I didn't choose to do this, and that I'd be so exhausted from fighting my feelings that I couldn't find the energy to do anything except get up and take care of the boys.

After I finished, my coach was quiet for a few moments, perhaps thinking about what I had said. Then she asked, "What happens when you do eventually fall into the darkness?"

I sat there in silence, thinking about her question. I had just described what happened whenever I fell into this depression, but that wasn't what she was talking about. Still, I wasn't sure how to respond. I hoped she would jump in and give me the answer. Instead, she watched me patiently as I tried to find it on my own. After several minutes, I realized what she meant. If this "fall into the darkness" had happened multiple times, I was finding a way out each time. I wasn't just living there. And every time I came out of the darkness, no matter if it took me days or weeks to do so, I would feel better, even renewed. That was the simple yet eye-opening answer.

My coach followed this up with another question, one I couldn't answer without her assistance: "If you felt better after going into the darkness, after letting grief and its mix of emotions take you, why do you fight it?"

Fear. That was why, I discovered. I fought it because of the fear. I was scared that if I didn't fight it, I wouldn't be able to get out. I was afraid I'd turn into one of those miserable people whose stories I read online, that I'd never learn how to carry the weight and continue living. I was scared to death of becoming that kind of person.

During that session, my coach helped me see I had no reason to fear the darkness. I had already spent weeks there without a hint of light breaking through, and I had made it out every time. I realized I couldn't fight the grief, and that was OK. The storm would always come, maybe not as often or for as long, but as long as love and grief were there, depression and darkness would be there too. I was afraid of something that hadn't happened, and probably wouldn't ever happen. Even though I had made the decision to live and find the light back on the coast in Bandon after Joe had died, I was still spending all my limited energy on fighting my feelings because I was scared. Now I knew there were healing, life, and peace in the darkness. It wasn't an enjoyable place to go, but it was a healthy one nonetheless.

So I stopped fighting the darkness. When I felt the storm coming, I would walk into it. I'd let myself feel horrible; I would cry, scream, sleep, and do whatever my body and my mind told me I needed to do. Sometimes the darkness would strike suddenly and unexpectedly, triggered by something I had seen or heard like an ambulance. When it did, I'd allow myself to sit there and cry. And by not fighting the darkness, I could escape it sooner. The storms were shorter, the light was easier to find, and I'd feel so much better afterward. The weight I had felt as a survivor—that need to be strong, suck it up, and move on—lifted away once I gave myself permission to feel shitty.

My coach also made me feel better about crying. With her help, I realized it was part of the darkness and also part of life. If I needed to go into the storm, no matter where I was, I needed to be comfortable with the tears that would fall. I didn't need to be ashamed, and I shouldn't try to hide them or wipe them away. I learned to acknowledge that, on some days, I just felt like crying; and rather than try to avoid tears in those situations, I needed to be open about it.

The trick was realizing that I couldn't control how others felt. They would respond to my actions, but I couldn't control what they would say or think about me. With my coach's help, I learned I was the only person I could control. Yes, I wanted to be kind and respectful, but I didn't need to care how others perceived my actions. So what if they thought I was making a mistake? Or if they pitied me or thought I was a victim? Or if they believed I never loved Joe because I was with Kyle? So what?

What was more important was that I felt confident in my decisions, that I took the time to look at my decisions and actions from every angle. I needed to believe in myself and have confidence. And through my coach's insight, I began to recover that confidence. I began to tell others, wherever I was, that I might cry, and I'd ask that they ignore it if I did. In those situations, saying it as a fact and not as something to be ashamed of made it easier to deal with my tears when they came. And if I warned people that it might happen, they weren't caught off guard by it and were able to respond in the way I had asked, which made me feel less judged or pitied. More often than not, the weight of having to keep myself from crying was lifted; and since I didn't feel as pressured, the tears didn't fall nearly as often.

One time, when I was driving to Bend for another session with my coach and watching other cars pass by, a different fear came to mind. It was a fear I hadn't voiced before. So when I sat in the cozy armchair in my coach's office, grasping a cup of warm tea just to have something to hold on to, I told her, "I'm scared I won't remember him."

"What are you scared of forgetting?" she asked, her gaze penetrating me in a way that made me feel like she could see into my soul and know my answers before I did.

"His voice," I said, looking out the small window. "His smile. The way he would move. His touch."

My coach settled back into her chair on the other side of the room. "So what happens if you do forget those things? Does that mean they weren't important to you?"

I paused for a moment, then let out a deep breath. "No."

"Does it mean you don't love him anymore?" she asked quietly.

"No," I repeated, slowly shaking my head. "I'll always love him."

"Does it mean he didn't love you?" she asked, tilting her head to the side and raising her eyebrows.

I sighed and looked into my cup of tea. "No."

"Love is what matters. You can't take that away," she said softly, leaning toward me and smiling. "Nothing can change that."

My coach was right. We have flawed memories, and we tend to forget things over time. But that's just life. Love, once felt, is something that can never be taken away. You can't lose love.

16

ONE OF MY FAVORITE BANDS, American Aquarium, has a song called "The World Is on Fire," written by the frontman BJ Barham. This particular verse from that song spoke to my soul when I first heard it:

> The load is heavy and the road is long
> And we've only begun to fight
> We just can't give in, we just can't give up
> We must go boldly into the darkness
> And be the light

This song gave words to the feelings I had begun to understand in my coaching sessions, but it took that understanding even further. There was something to be gained by going into the darkness. If you want to be more than what happened in your life, you have to choose it. You have to fight for it. To me, the song suggests that once you learn how to navigate the darkness, you can learn to be a light for others who've also found themselves there. I wanted to take my grief and learn to use it in that manner.

Before losing Joe, Brittany, and Grandpa Chuck, I wasn't capable of helping others with their grief because I was clueless about it. Now, as I was working through my grief, I learned more about it than I had ever thought possible. And with that knowledge came the realization that I could use what I had learned to help others and be their light. I could provide some hope and help them find happiness and live again despite the hand they had been dealt. This became my goal, and so I started a Soaring Spirits Regional Social Group for eastern Oregon. A few other women who had been widowed longer than I had been started coming, and we would have dinner together every month or so. This allowed me to be a resource for new people who were widowed in the Burns area so they wouldn't have to use so much energy to find resources on their own.

After I stopped being ashamed of my feelings and caring about what others were thinking about me or my grief, things got a lot better. I was able to grieve for Joe and continue piecing together the new me. I still went into the darkness, but I did it boldly, knowing it wouldn't last forever. Feeling confident in my ability to find the light, I continued to find ways to heal.

KYLE AND I ALSO became more public about our relationship, since I was able to truly embrace him. In July 2016, I went to Camp Widow® again, and Kyle agreed to go with me. While I participated in the workshops specific to widows, he found ways to entertain himself while making sure he was close by. That way, he would be there if I needed him.

One of the Camp Widow® sessions, however, was open to couples. So Kyle attended it with me, sitting next to me patiently as people shared their stories and the complications they experienced with being in a relationship while widowed. It gave us a chance to talk to other people who were dating after loss so we could discuss navigating relationships that had weird components, such as dead husbands. When we left that session, Kyle pulled me close and told me he was proud of me for coming to

Camp Widow® and happy to sit beside me. He supported and helped me whenever I needed it, both when I asked and when I was too stubborn to do so.

That summer, Kyle and I finally told Cody and Wade that we were dating. Up to that point, we had explained Kyle's presence by saying he was a friend and never did anything to suggest otherwise in front of the boys. Most of the time, we'd limit the time spent together to a few hours after the kids were asleep or the occasional days when friends or family would babysit. Slowly Kyle became a more regular fixture in my sons' lives. He never stayed at the house, but he was there more often during the day and spent more time with them. He was invited to family events—including events with Joe's family, since, after all, they were my family too—and participated in them willingly. The boys, who barely understood the concept of dating, were just excited to have someone they could jump on and play with more often.

On September 24, 2016, Kyle was playing games with Cody and Wade at my house when he brought out a small new puzzle. He gave it to me and suggested I help the boys put it together, but he wouldn't let us look at the box. As we worked on the puzzle, I smiled as I realized it was a puzzle made from pictures of the four of us. My heart started beating a little faster, and my face flushed with happiness as I began to see what was written on the puzzle.

When Kyle gave me the last piece, the words on the puzzle came together. I read them silently, and he got down on one knee next to me and my sons and repeated the words written on the puzzle. He asked me and the boys to marry him.

I looked at Kyle and felt my heart swell with love. He understood the fact that he wasn't just marrying me, but also Cody, Wade, and everything that came with us. Even better, he loved those boys as if they were his own blood. When I said yes, the boys erupted in loud cheers. Kyle slid an engagement ring, a blue sapphire held in a flower setting, onto my finger. It was perfect. I kissed Kyle as the boys hugged us.

While I didn't care so much about what people thought, I wanted to give everyone an opportunity to truly understand what had happened in my life. So I did something completely uncharacteristic. After Kyle and I told all our families, I announced our engagement on Facebook.

In that post, I shared what Joe had told me before he died, about how I would live, love, and find someone to love me and the boys if something happened to him. How, with that simple statement, he gave me a blessing and a gift, emphasizing his love, respect, and faith in me, not to just survive, but to thrive if he ever had to leave us. I wanted people to remember Joe. But more than that, I wanted them to know I still remembered him and still loved him. I would always love Joe and remember and honor everything we had, and yet I would look forward to loving someone in my new life.

Kyle and I were married on June 10, 2017, at Shore Acres, the place where I had found solace while grieving for Joe. It felt like a fitting tribute to marry Kyle there.

The wedding was simple, limited to only one hundred people. It took place on the lawn overlooking the formal gardens, with hundreds of flowers in bloom and the ocean rumbling in the distance. White chairs lined the aisle, with simple flowers decorating the ends. In each chair, we set a purple umbrella just in case the rain that was so common on the Oregon Coast made an appearance. That wasn't an issue, though. We were blessed that day with a light blue sky, white clouds occasionally floating by, and a warm breeze tinged with the smell of the ocean and the flowers surrounding us.

Next to the table where people could sign our guest book and leave cards, we placed a memorial table to honor the four people who were absent from the wedding and who we still grieved for: Kyle's dad, Bill; Brittany; Grandpa Chuck; and Joe. These four people helped shape me and Kyle into the people we had become. We loved and missed them. By displaying photos of them, they were still a part of the wedding. In that way, Joe was there, loving and supporting us despite not being there in person. In fact, his absence was the only reason the wedding was happening at all. Having him in a spot of honor brought my whole story together. Everyone I loved was at our wedding, in person or in spirit.

We had a simple ceremony with a certain amount of solemnity. In addition to my parents and Kyle's mom and brother, Joe's mom and her husband were also given a place of honor, walking down the aisle to start the ceremony. I wore a lace dress and held hands with five-year-old Cody and two-year-old Wade as we went down the aisle together, and the boys showered the guests with bubbles from their bubble guns instead of flower petals. They walked me to Kyle, and we stood in front of the pastor—the same pastor who had married me and Joe and then buried Joe. He had traveled from Burns with his family to officiate my and Kyle's wedding. In a way, this brought me full circle, and I liked the continuity of it. His presence offered compassion, understanding, and knowledge of what had led us to this moment in a way that no other pastor would have.

The vows we spoke included Cody and Wade, since we recognized we were becoming a family together. It wasn't just about Kyle and me; it was also about Cody and Wade. Kyle promised to be their dad and to take care of them no matter what, just as he promised to be my husband.

When it came time for the rings, we stood there under the

bright sun, with the boys beside us, as the pastor addressed our guests. "On Autumn's hand," he said, pointing to my left hand, which Kyle was holding tightly, "she already wears two rings on her ring finger. The first is a simple wedding band." He paused, smiling gently. "A wedding band that I watched get placed on her hand almost eight years ago. A wedding band that holds a lifetime of memories and, to this day, symbolizes an unbroken and never-ending love."

I met the pastor's eyes as he said this, and I knew we were both thinking about that September day when I had stood next to Joe.

"The second ring was not placed there as part of a ceremony," the pastor went on, "or even for a celebratory occasion. It is not one of happiness. It represents the loss of a husband. A widow's ring. But it is not there to remind her of grief or sadness."

As the pastor said this, I couldn't help but glance down at my rings, and I noticed other people were looking as well. I'd had a widow's ring made the first December after Joe died; it was Joe's Christmas present to me. It was a simple ring with five stones separated by white gold, representing the five years we were married. The stones alternated between sapphires (Joe's birthstone) and black diamonds to represent the loss. I wore the ring on the ring finger of my left hand, next to my wedding band and in honor of Joe. I wanted something that would be with me always. So the widow's ring was a physical symbol of my loss and pain, a "scar" that others could see, a visible way of telling my story.

"This ring," the pastor continued, "is there to remind Autumn that hope lives, even with loss. It is there to remind her that love does not stop with death but transcends space and time. It is there to remind her that love is not mutually exclusive. And it reminds her that she can treasure and honor her past while embracing the future." He paused at each point to allow what he said to sink in.

"She will always be Joe's widow. But today, she will also become Kyle's wife, as she embraces her future and a third ring finds its home upon her left hand."

There were tears of sadness and joy at our wedding. There was pain, happiness, and even laughter when Wade decided he had to pee and tried to do so right there in the grass in front of everyone. It did eventually rain during the reception, just enough for the guests to use the purple umbrellas. But it was light and brief, falling around us while the sun still shone on our faces. It was a cleansing, blessing rain.

I now wear three rings on my left ring finger: two wedding bands separated by a widow's ring. In our dining room, two wedding pictures look over our table, with a different man in each one. I'm proud of my life, even though it has been sad; and I won't hide away my love for either Joe or Kyle. It's important our boys know that both of their dads—the one here on earth, and the one in heaven—are part of our family. Family is created through bonds of love that never break, even when we're separated by death. Love never ends, and there's always room for more love.

17

KYLE AND I EMBRACED LIFE as two people who knew firsthand how quickly things can change. For our honeymoon, we made plans to go to Italy, leaving the boys with their grandparents. As we planned our trip, we continued settling into our new lives as a married couple. We fell into a routine and went to church regularly.

A few months after we married, we were at church when an older woman walked up the center aisle to take her regular place in the front row. She tripped when she was right next to me and Kyle, falling and hitting her head. Kyle and some of the other members of the congregation jumped to action to see what was wrong and administer first aid. It was determined that she might have hurt her hip, and they comforted her while they waited for the ambulance to come.

I had been fine up to that point, helping however I could but mostly staying out of the way. But when they called for the ambulance, I began to shake. My temperature plummeted, my heart pounded faster, and tears streamed from my eyes. I was sitting in church, but in my mind I was back on that road the night Joe had died. I was kneeling next to Joe, not the older woman, as I wondered why it was taking so long for the ambulance to arrive.

I was at a point in my grief where I knew it was OK to cry, and I didn't rush out to hide my tears. But I also didn't want to draw attention to myself. So I sat there quietly, keeping my head down, wiping my tears as I needed, and taking deep breaths as my wave of panic slowly receded. Once the paramedics took care of the woman and Kyle sat next to me and held my hand, I felt the tension fully leave me. Everything seemed better once he was beside me.

WHEN WE WENT ON our honeymoon in September 2017, we spent a lot of time enjoying each other and our ability to share conversation without interruption from the boys. We talked about everything, including our future together. Kyle and I both wanted him to legally adopt Cody and Wade. He was their dad now; they had both started calling him that not long after the wedding, but he would have been their dad even if they had chosen to call him Kyle. He loved them and would do anything for them.

It sounded so simple, but the process wasn't easy. Adoptions traditionally require changes to a child's birth certificate, specifically to replace the biological parent(s) with the adoptive parent(s) and to change the child's last name. But Kyle was adamant about keeping Joe on the birth certificates and not changing Cody's and Wade's names. Eventually we found a lawyer who could ensure a legal adoption without requiring such changes. The boys were Kyle's just as much as they were Joe's; blood didn't play a role in it. This was a legal truth as much as it was a commitment before God. When Kyle married me, he promised, with God as his witness, to take care of all of us. To me and Kyle, being married before God was proof that every word we had said in our vows was true, as God would know them to be. But when it came to legal guardianship of Cody and Wade, the law needed documentation.

During our honeymoon, Kyle and I also decided that, while we were happy with our family exactly as it was, we wanted to add one more member: a baby who would have Kyle's last name. We knew there was a risk I would have a miscarriage, since I had a history of them. So if I didn't get pregnant, or if we lost the baby, we wouldn't keep trying. But we agreed we wanted one more, to just see what would happen.

God blessed us, however, with a healthy pregnancy and a beautiful baby girl. Rylee Marie Jackson was born at 1:48 p.m. on July 15, 2018, almost a week after her due date. She was much more stubborn than her brothers, who had both come early. Throughout the entire pregnancy, I knew she was strong, since her punches and kicks caused me more discomfort than either of her brothers had. She came out ready to take on the world.

Not only was Rylee strong, but she was also perfect and gorgeous, everything we ever could have dreamed of. She was big and healthy, and it was love at first sight for all four of us. We spent the afternoon in the hospital, showing her off to family and friends. And unlike both of her brothers, she latched on like a champ and nursed with no issue. Cody and Wade were awestruck by her and her big blue eyes, which watched them as they held her carefully with Kyle's help. She was calm, happy, and not at all fussy despite being thrust into a bright and different world.

While Rylee thrived, however, I continued to bleed. In order to ensure it would stop properly, I needed to be transported to Bend via ambulance. However, Rylee was less than twenty-four hours old and needed to stay in Burns so she could be monitored before being discharged. So, much to our disappointment, we had to separate temporarily. The boys went home with their aunt and uncle, I took an ambulance to Bend, and Kyle stayed with Rylee. A few hours after I left, Rylee was discharged. Kyle bundled her up and took her to Bend to join me. She took it in stride, just as she had done with everything else so far.

A few days later, once we were all home together, the four of us finally had the opportunity to spoil Rylee. Her big brothers especially enjoyed this. She would stare at Cody and Wade and watch them as they ran around, trying to find things she liked and persuade her to grab hold of the toys they gathered around her. Kyle and I would take turns holding her, and we'd find ourselves hypnotized by her beautiful eyes and the attention she gave us. The boys would lie on the floor with her, talking and playing with her.

When Rylee was old enough, she would grab her brothers' fingers and squeeze them tightly. Cody and Wade would light up with excitement and ask for pictures to document the moment. When it was time to change her diaper, Wade was always the first one there. He loved to ready the new diaper, make sure wipes were available, and take the trash for us. Both boys took great pride in caring for their little sister and would tell everyone they could about her and the things she was doing.

During those moments, when I'd lie on the floor with Kyle and our sons as we admired and loved our daughter, I was so content. It wasn't because I had moved on from losing Joe and other people I loved; that pain and the holes each loss had created in my heart were still there. But I could be happy simply because I chose to feel that way and to not allow trauma to determine how my life would be. I chose to live on in spite of what I had suffered, because the loved ones I had lost would want no less for me. I never thought I'd remarry or have another child; and when I did, I was elated.

WHEN RYLEE WAS ABOUT a month old, we took a family trip to the Eagle Cap Wilderness in northeastern Oregon. This was our first camping trip as a family of five. Rylee was able to enjoy some time in nature, watch her brothers learn to fly fish, and stare into the campfire. She would move her head to follow the birds or look at the wind blowing through the trees. Recently Rylee had begun to smile; and when she did, it was a big, full smile that made her eyes crinkle with happiness. So, of course, the rest of us spent hours coaxing one more smile out of her, and she was usually more than happy to give us what we wanted. We valued this trip and the memories we made together so much; it became the first of many we would plan.

As summer went on, we continued to grow as a family. When Rylee was around two months old, we took her to the local county fair, which was one of Cody and Wade's favorite events. She watched her first parade and was shocked by the lights and noise from the fire engines and police cars. Cody and Wade showered her with the candy they gathered from each passing float, not caring that she was too young to eat it. They just wanted to share what they had with her, which was a sign of true sibling love. At the fair, Rylee was loved on by everyone and passed around to any friends and relatives who called dibs on her.

As I sat in the grandstand and watched the rodeo, I thought about all the times I had come to the county fair in the past and sat in these bleachers. When Joe and I were first dating, we would attend the rodeo together if he wasn't working. If he was, I would often come myself, bring a book for company, and enjoy the festivities alone, anxiously waiting for when Joe would join me.

For a small rural town like Burns, the county fair is the social event of the year. People come from out of town to participate in events or be a spectator, but mostly to visit with friends or family they haven't seen for a while. The county fair was where Joe had first introduced me to many of his friends and other people he had grown up with. Now, as I was sitting in the stands with Kyle, Rylee, Cody, and Wade, I realized how much time had passed since that first fair. My life had changed so much in just a few years. Yet it was still hard to believe that Joe was no longer there with me, and that Kyle and Rylee were.

As I watched Cody win the belt buckle in Mutton Bustin', I couldn't help but think how happy Joe would be for his oldest son. I carried on a whole conversation with my first husband in my head while smiling with Cody over his win. Joe may not have been there, but I had no doubt that he was proud wherever he was, and I was proud of myself for being able to miss Joe in that moment and not fall into overwhelming sadness. I had grown in my grief so much in the past couple of years that I could acknowledge the sad thoughts but focus on and enjoy the present.

Cody and I walked back to the grandstand, and my son stood tall with a big smile on his face as strangers congratulated him on his win and asked to see his buckle. While he was happy to share it, I knew all he really wanted to do was to show it to Rylee.

After the rodeo, Kyle and I took the boys on some carnival rides. Rylee's eyes were big as she watched all the flashing lights and moving pieces. A smile would spread across her face whenever her brothers suddenly appeared, spinning on the ride.

We had a busy day at the fair, but Rylee only cried a little to let us know when she was hungry. Most of the day, she was a trouper as we shuffled her around in the heat. She was easy to take care of and easy to love, since she had already stolen the hearts of the four of us as well as her aunts, uncles, grandparents, and friends of the family. Many of us had suffered so much loss, and Rylee had become a symbol of recovery from grief and sadness, the embodiment of moving forward. She was a glowing spot of happiness in our lives, and I felt blessed by God that He had allowed me the gifts and love I had found in her, Kyle, Cody, and Wade.

Rylee developed a bubbly, cooing laugh that encouraged us all to chuckle along with her. It matched her smile and big blue eyes, and it would always start on one side of her mouth, giving it a wonderful lopsided effect. Then it would spread across her entire face with deep gurgles that erupted from her little throat.

A few weeks after the county fair, the four of us took a family trip to the Oregon Coast. There, Rylee experienced the ocean, played in the sand, rode a train, and toured the Tillamook Creamery with us. She seemed to enjoy watching Cody and Wade fly kites and napping in the arms of whoever was holding her.

The coast trip was followed by a weekend in eastern Oregon for Kyle's brother's wedding. While Kyle performed his duties as best man, I took Cody, Wade, and Rylee on a walk. The boys ran around me and Rylee in the bright sun and picked every golden dandelion they could find. When their hands were full, they would run back to Rylee and gently place them in her lap. The stroller overflowed with flowers, and my heart with love and happiness. When Joe had died, I had doubted I would love or be happy again, but life and God had given me gifts. Despite the horrific losses, I was so happy with what I had been given. I couldn't imagine life without Rylee in it now. She was meant to be there, even though I would find myself confused by that thought, because her being there was only possible because Joe had died.

At the wedding, Rylee sat with me in the front row, watching quietly and with a patience many babies didn't have. Meanwhile, Kyle, Cody, and Wade played their parts in the ceremony. Afterward, we were lucky enough to have some family pictures taken, the first photographs of all five of us together. The boys were so cute in their black cowboy hats, jeans, white shirts, purple suspenders, and bow ties. Kyle looked handsome in his jeans and vest, and Rylee wore a pink tulle skirt that she loved to grab. The picture captured us in a time of pure happiness.

RYLEE WAS AN EASY, happy baby. She was amazing and wonderful, a blessing. At her worst, she would cry, though not too loudly and only for ten minutes or so. But usually, she was at her best, doling out smiles and laughs. As she grew older, she would giggle and squirm, look at us with her big blue eyes, and encourage us to play with her more. She was so filled with joy that she would often take a break from nursing, her mouth still filled with milk, to smile and laugh. The milk would run out of her mouth, soaking me in the process.

One of Rylee's favorite things was when her dad would help her "jump." They would sit in his chair, and Kyle would hold Rylee up, her legs bent gently under her. As soon as she made any movement with her legs, he would jump her high into the air above his head; and her gurgling laugh would fill the air until she touched back down, ready to do it again. I snuck a video of one of these moments once and would watch it whenever I needed a laugh or a reminder of how blessed I was to have them both in my life. Because despite the trauma, loss, and pain we had suffered, life was good. Actually, life was great. We were together as a family. The five of us were taking time to enjoy each other and trying not to stress out over small things.

18

THE PERIOD OF JOY WAS short-lived. At the end of October, our family came down with mild colds. Cody and Wade had them first, then Kyle and I caught them. They weren't much, just some sniffles and mild sore throats. The four of us still went to work, school, and everywhere else.

Eventually Rylee caught the cold. She had a runny nose, was a little fussier, and didn't eat as well, which we attributed to a sore throat. She had no other issues at first; she was still smiling, laughing, and playing with the boys. But after two days, it became difficult for her to nurse or drink from a bottle. We grew concerned about dehydration and took her to the doctor the next morning. During the apppointment, the doctor noticed Rylee's dehydration as well as some weakness when Rylee tried to hold her head up.

While we had reason to be concerned, the doctor assured us that Rylee's condition was easily treatable. She sent us to the emergency room so Rylee could be rehydrated through an IV. But after an hour or so, with Rylee crying weakly throughout, the doctors hadn't been able to get an IV in her. It turned out she had very small veins and rather chubby extremities, making her veins hard to locate. Rather than continuing to poke at her, we were admitted to the hospital so Rylee could be given a nasogastric tube, which enters through the nose and travels down the esophagus into the stomach. Using that, we were able to feed her a few milliliters of formula every fifteen minutes throughout the night.

Every few hours, Kyle and I would take turns holding Rylee, feeding her, and watching her sleep. We arranged for someone to babysit Cody and Wade; and the boys visited their sister that night, giving her hugs and kisses and praying she would get better and come home soon. We also let everyone know she was doing OK. It was just a cold, we told them. Nothing serious. We were only in the hospital to get fluids into her.

Rylee was monitored throughout the night. Kyle and I kept track of what was going on and how she was acting. The nurses came in every two hours to weigh her diapers, which she had started to fill as she was rehydrated. They would listen to her heart and lungs and check her blood oxygen levels and temperature.

The next morning, Rylee was looking much better, but she still wasn't eating on her own or holding her head up as well as usual. She was still alert and responsive, waving her arms, kicking her feet, and giving us her trademark smile, though it wasn't quite as radiant. The doctors were concerned about the weakness, so they decided to test her for meningitis using a lumbar puncture. It was a simple procedure that they would do in her room, though Kyle and I would have to step out for a few minutes.

When it was time for the procedure, Kyle and I moved Rylee over to the crib by the window. We were worried about her having to go through the lumbar puncture, and the possibility that she had meningitis scared us. Since both of us were anxious, we took turns telling her we loved her and how the procedure might hurt but wouldn't be too bad. We told her that she was strong and tough and that we'd be back as soon as it was over. She rewarded us with a smile just before we left the room.

Kyle and I walked slowly into the waiting room. I was nervous because we couldn't be in the room with her, and I knew Kyle was as well. We had both heard stories about how painful meningitis could be. At the same time, we were glad she was being tested for it now, before it got worse. If she did have meningitis, we hoped they could treat her for it right away.

We had just sat down when a Code Blue for Rylee's room was called out over the hospital loudspeaker. I had been in enough hospitals and seen enough TV to know what Code Blue meant: Rylee's heart had stopped beating.

Everything went in slow motion then. Kyle and I both looked at each other. Before we had finished processing the announcement, a nurse came to grab us. She brought us to the hallway outside Rylee's room, where we tried to stay out of the way as doctors and nurses ran into the room and performed compressions on her chest as she lay in the crib.

We stood there and waited . . . and prayed.

The strange thing was, I was so angry that this was happening and that God was letting this happen, but I continued to pray for Him to heal Rylee. I prayed that this wasn't happening, not again. In my mind, I screamed at God, threatening Him as sobs racked my body and tears clouded my vision. But I prayed anyway. It doesn't matter how much you hate God; I don't even think it matters if you believe in God or not. When something scary and traumatic is happening and there's nothing you can do to fix it or make it better, it's human nature to pray. Sometimes it's the only thing you can do besides waiting helplessly.

So I prayed, and Kyle prayed. His lips moved, and an occasional whisper came from them. I knew his prayers matched mine. Our friends arrived and prayed around us. The hospital staff joined us in prayer when they could. Doctors and nurses continued running in and out of the room, looking worried. Any staff members who weren't needed in the room held us and tried to comfort us. One nurse lowered me to the floor when my legs gave out. We prayed that this hell we were now living wasn't real, that everything would be OK and God would help Rylee. We prayed for a miracle.

We sat there in the hall outside Rylee's room as the hospital focused on saving her life. I curled up next to Kyle as we clung to each other. Eventually, even as the doctors continued working on Rylee, a nurse came and told us the unexplainable: When the doctor had rolled Rylee onto her side to look at her spine before beginning the lumbar puncture, Rylee's heart had arrested. That was it. No heartbeat, no breathing. She had simply died.

The doctors and nurses continued to work on Rylee, and we continued to wait. Kyle and I called our families, including Joe's, to let them know what was going on. The relatives we spoke to immediately headed to the hospital. In the meantime, we stayed by her door, pacing when we could stand, and crying. We listened to the noises and voices in the room behind us, trying to understand what was happening. And we held each other for all we were worth. Tears streamed down not just our faces, but also the faces of staff members.

Still, the doctors and nurses worked on Riley. The longer they worked, the harder we prayed. And yet the longer they worked, the lower the odds were for Rylee's survival.

About forty minutes after Code Blue was called, Rylee's pediatrician and the doctor who was in the room when Rylee had coded came out of the room and kneeled on the floor in front of us. Shock and fog had settled over me by then, so I don't remember what the pediatrician said. But it didn't matter. Kyle and I both knew that, at this point, the odds of the doctors saving Rylee were next to none. And if we did get her back, the risk of her having brain damage was high.

I asked the doctors how much longer they would work on Rylee before giving up. It had already felt like a lifetime since her heart had first stopped, but we held on to hope. We didn't want them to stop until they brought her back. That was what my heart wanted, but my brain was telling me we might have to decide to let her go.

The two doctors sat on the floor with us, tears in their eyes. They told us they would continue working on Rylee until we told them to stop. And I believed them. We knew probably half of the people who were working on her. This was more than just a job to them; this was someone in their community, and they would do everything they could to help her. But these doctors were out here with us because they hadn't been able to resuscitate our daughter so far. Kyle and I looked at them, then at each other. Neither of us wanted to give them the order that would end with us losing Rylee for good.

How do you do that? How do you tell a doctor it's OK to stop trying to save your daughter? I didn't have the words to give the answer I knew we'd have to give.

Then something changed. We all glanced up as the atmosphere in Rylee's room shifted. The room had grown quiet as the doctors and nurses continued to work on her. Now, the activity had suddenly picked back up. Doctors and nurses were rushing in and out. Rylee's heart was beating again.

Now it was no longer about bringing Rylee back from death, but about keeping her alive. Just because she had a heartbeat didn't mean she would recover—or even live, especially since no one knew what was wrong with her. But at least for that moment, she was alive and fighting. We hadn't lost her completely, so we still had hope.

Tears once again rushed down my and Kyle's faces. This time, they were tears of joy and thankfulness. It seemed like God had answered our prayers and given us our miracle. We wanted nothing more than to rush in and hold Rylee and talk to her. But we held each other and stayed by the door, pushing against the wall so we could hear what was going on while staying out of the way.

Real life isn't like life on TV, where everything is better just because the patient has a heartbeat. Rylee remained unconscious, and the doctors and nurses worked to stabilize her. She was placed on a ventilator, and arrangements were made to transport her via air ambulance to a children's hospital in Boise, about 200 miles away.

In the meantime, Kyle and I tried to figure out what to tell Cody and Wade. They knew we were in the hospital with Rylee and she was sick. So we told the boys her condition had worsened and we were taking her to a bigger hospital. We left them with their uncle (Joe's brother) and aunt, with directions to protect the boys from the seriousness of the situation and to follow their regular schedule. Routine was especially helpful for Cody, as I had learned after we had lost Joe; and I wanted to continue that as much as possible. We wanted them to go to school and have fun trick-or-treating in their dinosaur costumes, and not to worry about their sister more than they needed to.

After a few hours, the trauma team from the children's hospital arrived. We stood outside the door and listened to their briefing. Kyle and I were given a few minutes to see Rylee and talk to her. Then my daughter and I were loaded into an ambulance, driven to the airport, and put on a small medical transport plane with a pilot and two nurses. I took a small seat on the plane before Rylee was brought aboard on a stretcher and locked into place next to me. I saw her in her unnatural stillness, but I couldn't touch her. The nurses sat in two seats next to her so they could monitor her.

As the nurses worked on Rylee, their conversation was minimal but their expressions spoke volumes. Rylee wasn't as stable as they had hoped, but there was very little they could do in the plane.

We were only in the air for about forty-five minutes, but it was the longest and scariest flight of my life. All I wanted to do was to hold my daughter and scream at them to help her. But all I could do was sit there quietly, out of their way, and pray.

Things continued to unfold in slow motion. An ambulance was waiting for us at the airport in Idaho, and we were quickly whisked away into Boise traffic toward the downtown hospital. I knew everyone was working as quickly and efficiently as they could. But when it comes to the people you love, it's never enough.

When we arrived at the pediatric intensive care unit (PICU) in the children's hospital, a team of doctors and nurses were ready to take over Rylee's care. I stayed outside the room, watching through the window as they worked. Due to her small veins, it took a number of hours before she was fully stabilized.

Still, I could do nothing but sit, stare, and pray. I wanted to help, but I didn't have the medical knowledge to do anything. I wanted to comfort Rylee, even though she wasn't awake. I wanted to hold her, talk to her, let her know she wasn't alone. But with the doctors and nurses surrounding her, there was no room for me next to her. I wanted to pace the floor, but I couldn't bear to be any further from her than possible. So I fell back to what I knew and what I had done in Burns. This time, though, I was alone. No friends, no family, no doctors or nurses I knew, and no Kyle.

After a while, the hospital chaplain came to talk to me, but it was impossible for me to carry on a conversation. The stress of the last few hours had taken its toll on me, and I was using the last bit of my mental capacity to pray and to keep from falling apart in the middle of the PICU. I answered her questions, my voice sounding empty and hollow. In the meantime, the doctors and nurses were unable to stabilize Rylee, determine what had caused her cardiac arrest in the first place, or tell me she would be OK. And soon I found the hope I had felt back in Burns, when Rylee's heart had started beating again, was fading away.

About four hours after Rylee and I had left Burns, Kyle, my sister, Kyle's brother, and his wife arrived at the hospital around the same time. Kyle came back with me to Rylee's room, and the others went to a family waiting room. Once Rylee was stabilized and fewer staff members were needed in her room, we were able to go inside and look at her.

What we saw both shocked and scared us. Rylee was swelling all over, including her face. Her eyelids were unable to fully cover her beautiful blue eyes. She looked so different from the little girl we knew. And as much as Kyle and I wanted to be there for Rylee, it didn't seem like she was there anymore.

When the nurses took her for a CT scan, we went back to the family waiting room. We told our siblings that we didn't want them to see her, and that we needed some time before going back to her room. We knew we would go back eventually, but seeing her that way was so hard, and we didn't want our families to have that picture of Rylee in their head. We had hoped and prayed so hard that she would eventually heal and be OK. But this was the first time since the doctors had brought her back that I really doubted it. All of my earlier hope had disappeared. The emptiness and the darkness were overwhelming.

As I sat in the small room, holding Kyle's hand, I felt my heart racing. I stared at the door, but I didn't really see it. I only saw Rylee's face, which was now so different from the happy, healthy one I knew intimately. A weight seemed to push against my chest, making it hard to breathe, and my head began to spin. I thought I might pass out, but I needed to be there for Rylee. So I stubbornly pushed away the promise of oblivion and forced myself to sit still and regulate my breathing, silently praying and grasping Kyle's hand as if it was the only thing that was keeping me sane.

We had prepared ourselves for the worst. So when the doctor came and said he didn't see the brain swelling he had expected, we were surprised. The minimal amount of swelling on her brain meant she might wake up. It was still a small chance, but it was enough to hope.

We needed all the prayers we could get, so we asked for them on social media. Many people knew Rylee was sick and what had happened in Burns, but we chose not to explain the situation so we could protect Cody and Wade from the details. As soon as we posted the request on our pages and in all the groups I was a member of, the prayers started pouring in. Our message reached people across the United States, and it wasn't long before prayers started coming from England, Australia, and other places around the world. They were simple messages to let us know the senders were praying for Rylee. They were praying for a miracle and would keep praying as long as we needed them to.

Kyle and I also decided that Cody and Wade didn't need to see Rylee in the hospital in her current state. They didn't need that memory. We didn't know if it was the right choice, but it was the best we could do at that time. We didn't want the boys to have to deal with that worry or pain until we were more certain of the outcome, and then we would tell them.

Later, we found out that some kids at school had told Cody that Rylee had died. He didn't really believe them, and he didn't tell anyone what he had heard. But it still worried him. It still breaks my heart today to think of a six-year-old holding that fear to himself. Even though we didn't know what Cody and Wade had heard around town, we did what we could to calm their worries without lying to them. So when we talked to them, we just told them she was still really sick and everyone was doing the best they could to take care of her. We could tell they were still worried, especially Cody, whose voice quivered as he tried not to cry. But it was all we could do.

Late that night, after a few hours of stabilization and medication, Rylee's swelling decreased. She began to look like our little girl again. In fact, if I ignored the tubes and machines she was hooked up to, she looked almost normal—except for the stillness. Even when sleeping, Rylee would move her body. Now, only her chest moved up and down regularly as the ventilator gave her the oxygen she needed.

Kyle and I set up camp on the couch in her room and allowed our relatives to visit Rylee. One of the nurses who had checked on her earlier covered her with pink blankets. It helped to break up the white sterility of the hospital bed and make things more comfortable for us as well as Rylee. It also showed us that, for the nurses, Rylee wasn't just another patient. She was a baby girl who had a name, was loved, and deserved something pretty. I began to notice the love in that room that night: from me and Kyle, our families, and the nurses who took everything in stride, answering a million questions, keeping us all informed, and simply taking amazing care of Rylee. They would talk to her, move her, apologize for poking her, fix her hair, and bathe her. Every nurse who worked on Rylee treated her with love, and it was beautiful.

19

KYLE AND I SPENT A sleepless night on the small couch in Rylee's room. We took turns standing next to her bed, holding her hand, stroking her face, and talking to her, letting her know she wasn't alone and we would always be there for her. The nurses and doctors came in periodically to check on her, adjust her medications, and run some tests. Overnight, Rylee's swelling continually decreased until the beautiful little face we loved looked normal. I hoped that was a good sign; maybe she would wake up and come back to us.

The next morning, a dull light seeped in through the small window, and the nurses went through their shift change. A new doctor, Dr. D, took over Rylee's care. The nurses told us we would recognize him when he walked in.

"Just imagine a full-grown Shaggy from *Scooby-Doo* wearing scrubs," they told us, smiling and laughing. "He may look like Shaggy, but he is a great doctor."

Their description didn't inspire a lot of confidence, but it aroused our curiosity. And when Dr. D walked in, we understood the comparison. His hair was long, hanging below his ears; and his mustache and full beard covered the bottom half of his face. But his blue eyes were kind, with laugh lines around them. So not only did we know who this man was when he entered the room, but we also knew he was more than that description. He was calm, knowledgeable, and caring. He sat down, looked directly at me and Kyle, and gently laid out the facts. This was the first time someone at the hospital had done that with us.

Dr. D explained that they still didn't know what had caused Rylee to go into cardiac arrest and had been running tests to figure it out. But so far, all the tests had come back negative. In the meantime, Rylee's body functions had continued to improve. Her heart was beating stronger and with good rhythm, and her lungs were working better, with the supplemental oxygen decreased to natural levels. However, her brain wasn't working.

At the same time, Dr. D reminded us it had taken the doctors in Burns a long time to get Rylee's heart going again. Once they did, it had been difficult to stabilize her. He told us gently but clearly what would happen as we moved forward: The doctors in Boise would keep Rylee stabilized and would try to figure out what had happened to her heart, but it was possible that, despite the results of the CT scan, she had brain damage. It was also likely that she wouldn't survive.

"However," Dr. D added with a shrug, "the brain is resilient, especially in children. It's possible she could recover. I do not think that is likely, but we will do everything we can. We really just have to wait and see what happens."

Then Dr. D talked with us about Rylee. He wanted to learn about her and provided me and Kyle with whatever support he could offer. He also asked us about our religion. When we said we were Christian, he offered to stand over Rylee's bed with us and pray for her. It was an inspiring combination of science and faith. From our conversation with Dr. D, I knew he was going to do everything he could to help Rylee come home to us. But I also knew he felt science would only get us so far and we would need a miracle from God for Rylee to recover. His admission that we needed God made me feel better about my constant praying. It was all I could do, but maybe it would be worthwhile.

After Dr. D prayed over Rylee with us, he asked if we would be willing to accept a gift from his sister. She had prayed over some blankets and attached to each one a handwritten bible verse in beautiful script, then asked Dr. D to give them to families who needed them the most. He felt that we were that family, and we said yes. He left and soon returned with a beautiful blue blanket trimmed with white. It was one of the most thoughtful gifts I ever received, one that gave comfort during a time of pain and was made with love for a complete stranger.

Rylee's next test was a twenty-four-hour electroencephalogram (EEG) to monitor for brain function. They placed electrodes all over her scalp, and the wires were connected to a computer. A camera was placed to record any activity that occurred.

As the doctors ran more tests, more loved ones arrived: Kyle's mom, Joe's mom and her husband, cousins from my family and Kyle's, my brother and his family, our pastor and his wife, and one of Kyle's best friends. My parents, aunt, and uncle even returned early from a trip to Israel. Eventually, the family waiting room and Rylee's room were overflowing with love and support as we prayed and waited. I had felt alone when I first entered the PICU, but now I was overwhelmed with emotion because I was surrounded by friends and family who loved us and hoped with us. So many people had interrupted their lives to come to our sides as we waited to learn our daughter's fate. It was a reminder of how truly blessed we were despite the horrible situation.

Dr. D helped keep our minds off our worry. We talked about his little girl, who loved pink, sparkles, and glitter. "You know, I hate glitter," he told us with a glint in his eye. "Glitter is like the herpes of do-it-yourself. Once you have it, you can never get rid of it."

Kyle, Dr. D, and I burst out laughing then. It was such a nice break from the seriousness of the situation.

In many ways, all the past losses and experiences I had been through before helped me understand that talking and laughing didn't mean I loved Rylee any less. They also didn't mean I wasn't doing everything I could for her or I wasn't worried sick about her. Instead, I had learned that I should take any happiness I can, under any situation, because it may be short-lived, and that laughing is so much more healing and comforting than crying.

While we were at the hospital, one of the nurses told us that Rylee's name means *courageous*, which was so fitting. Rylee had always been strong and brave. She was fighting her battle as courageously as possible. So she became our courageous miracle.

Also, as we prayed for her, we decided she loved butterflies and the color purple. I'm still not sure where either came from. Maybe we thought of butterflies because my sister had given Rylee a blanket with butterflies on it after she was born. And maybe we picked purple because it fit her smooth complexion so well and brought out the blue in her eyes. Regardless of the reasons for those choices, we wanted to give Rylee more than her short life had allowed for her. We wanted her to have her own preferences.

While Kyle and I received comfort from our family and the hospital staff, we mostly found comfort in each other. We always sat next to each other and held hands. We encouraged each other to eat, though it was difficult. We tried to sleep, since the hospital had given us a bedroom, but it was impossible to leave Rylee. So we would nap when exhaustion took over, crammed together on the couch. But no matter what happened, we were doing this together. Whenever we were separated, I would feel much worse, so I avoided going anywhere without Kyle. There was even some (partially joking) discussion about going to the bathroom together, because even that much space between us felt too far. In the end, we would stand on opposite sides of the door, but we still didn't like it.

With little to distract us in the hospital, Kyle and I got to know the different nurses and specialists as they checked on Rylee. We shared stories and pictures of her before she got sick and talked to them about medical stuff as well as themselves. We asked them where they were from and how long they had worked at the hospital. Some of the nurses had only been in the PICU for a few months. Others had been there for years. A few nurses were local, and some had come from the East Coast. One was from Wales, and she patiently explained the difference between Great Britain and the United Kingdom.

Rylee was never alone in that room. Friends and family were always touching her, talking to her, and reading to her. There was always love. It was better when lots of people were there, since we were all scared. But together we were able to talk and even laugh. We had all gone through grief and learned to let ourselves laugh or smile whenever the opportunity arose. Plus, if Rylee were still there and aware of what was happening in her room, wouldn't the sound of happiness comfort her? Why not grasp onto joy whenever you can, even if tears are running down your face?

ONCE THE EEG WAS complete, we knew as soon as Dr. D walked in that the news wasn't good. He put his chair directly in front of me and Kyle so he could look right at us and hold our hands. He explained that, over the past twenty-four hours, Rylee's brain had showed absolutely no signs of activity. Our daughter wasn't going to wake up.

Dr. D then explained the next step. Once we were ready, we

would need to test for brain death. Since the EEG had already showed no activity, only one test for brain death was required. However, we could choose to do two tests twenty-four hours apart. By giving us this option, he was also giving us a choice, a small bit of control.

Kyle and I wanted to give Ryleer every possible chance to survive and give God an opportunity for a miracle. We chose to do the two tests, with the first one occurring as soon as possible.

That night, we went to the small bedroom the hospital had provided us, leaving Rylee in the care of our family members. Sleep was hard to come by, even though we were exhausted. But we needed just a few hours alone to figure out how in the hell to do this. As we laid there in the dark, our arms and legs intertwined, with only my periodic sobs breaking the silence, we made a pact to do this together and survive. Many marriages don't survive the loss of a child, especially with guilt, blame, and isolation all playing roles. But Kyle and I agreed to not blame each other and to do our best not to feel guilty—or, more realistically, to not drown in it and let it destroy us. We also agreed not to hide our pain from each other. My pain was Kyle's pain, and we were in this together. We would cry together, suffer together, and—more importantly—heal together.

At that point, we knew in our hearts and souls that Rylee wasn't coming home. We wanted to give her the benefit of the doubt and all the time she needed to recover, but we didn't think she was there anymore. Our hope for her survival was gone, but we still had another hope. If we couldn't have our miracle, then maybe Rylee could be a miracle for others. So we asked the doctor about organ donation.

For Kyle and I, it wasn't much of a discussion. We didn't want any other families to go through what we had been going through.

Even though Rylee's brain refused to recover, her body was still strong. We didn't know if it would even be possible, since we didn't know what had caused her cardiac arrest. But we needed to try.

Dr. D contacted the transplant bank, and soon a team of people arrived to help us fill out forms, walk us through the process, and determine if Rylee could donate. What she could give was limited due to her size. However, she was just over the minimum weight required for donating organs, specifically her liver, kidneys, and heart. She wasn't able to donate her corneas, but even if she wEre, Kyle and I wouldn't have felt comfortable about it. Those big, beautiful, happy eyes that had always smiled would only be hers.

The donor team was also very clear that, because of Rylee's size and type A positive blood, they didn't know if there would be any matching recipients. It would have been hard to willingly donate her organs only to discover no patients could receive them. But from my perspective, it also meant it was more likely that the people who shared Rylee's blood type or small size had less hope to receive an organ in time. They had probably been told the likelihood of finding matches was slim. By that logic, this gift from our daughter would mean so much more to them.

The donor team began searching for matches and transplant doctors who were willing to take the risk without knowing what had caused Rylee's cardiac arrest. It didn't happen quickly or all at once, like things often do in medical dramas on TV. Kyle and I were told it would take a minimum of twenty-four hours, but most likely forty-eight to seventy-two hours. The donor team needed to perform not just a simple blood test, but rather different tests for different organs. Each member of the team would work a full twenty-four-hour shift to confirm these matches.

The first organ we received a match for was Rylee's kidneys. Then the donor team found preliminary matches for her liver and heart. Rylee had potential to be a miracle for three people, three families. As cliché as it might sound, the news really was a silver lining. The thought of our daughter saving others took some of the sharpness off our grief. It was our own little glimmer of light, shining in the darkness that had overtaken our lives.

In the meantime, the hospital continued to test Rylee to understand what had happened to her. But all the tests, including the one for meningitis, came back negative. The doctor who was with Rylee when she had coded at the hospital in Burns had been in touch with the doctors at the children's hospital, eventually asking them to run other tests, including one for botulism. Even though the doctors at the children's hospital didn't think Rylee's symptoms matched up very well with botulism, they agreed to perform the test. It was one of the last possibilities anyone could think of.

Rylee went through the brain death protocol as planned. As expected, both tests showed no response, and she was officially declared brain-dead. The coroner was required to sign off on the organ donation, and an investigator talked to me and Kyle as well as the doctor and nurses to help determine the cause and mode of death and whether a full autopsy was needed. The investigator didn't feel there would be any issues in continuing with the donation. The goal was no longer recovery for Rylee, but rather maintenance of her organs. The transplant bank, whose staff consisted of nurses, took over Rylee's care and associated expenses.

At this point, the only thing that was helping me and Kyle make it through the day was knowing Rylee could be a miracle for other people. Despite not knowing the cause of her death, we knew other doctors wanted her organs, even after they had been briefed on her case and understood all the uncertainty and questions still surrounding it.

A few hours later, though, Dr. D and the staff from the

transplant bank came in, looking sad and worried. They informed us that the coroner was refusing to release Rylee for donation. He felt the risk of not knowing what had caused Rylee's cardiac arrest was too high.

That moment—not the moment when we were told Rylee was really gone—was our lowest point on this journey. It felt like the one thing that was giving us comfort, the idea that Rylee's life could save others, was being taken from us.

I cried at that moment. I may have even yelled. Only Dr. D's calmness kept me from completely collapsing.

"Don't give up hope yet," he said, hugging me and Kyle. "I am going to call and talk to the coroner, see if I can figure out what his issue is. Once we know what the problem is, maybe we can figure something out where he would allow Rylee to still donate."

That was something I could focus on. If Rylee could donate even one organ, if she could save just one life, it would give some meaning to my and Kyle's loss. If Rylee could help one family and prevent them from experiencing the hell we were going through then, it would give us something to hold onto.

"I am at peace," Dr. D said, making eye contact with each of us and grasping our hands. "I have prayed on this, and I feel in my heart it will work out. Trust me, and give me just a little bit of time."

"OK," I said, feeling some of the panic leave my body. Dr. D's presence and insistence that it would work out gave me some hope that it would. It made me believe, even just a little, that he could fix it, that he could give us this one small victory in a war we had already lost.

Once again, Kyle and I sat and waited with our daughter while Dr. D went to bat for us. Both of us were awed by this man who officially was no longer Rylee's doctor but whose compassion and support for us were evident. It meant the world to us.

After a few hours, Dr. D was able to determine the coroner's major concern. Rylee may have had acute flaccid myelitis (AFM), a rare but serious neurological condition with symptoms similar to polio. The coroner didn't want to risk spreading that kind of illness by agreeing to the organ donation. And we completely understood his concern. We wanted to save parents from losing their children, not expedite that loss by infecting the child with an illness.

While the coroner's concern was legitimate, Dr. D still had good news: He had convinced the coroner to test Rylee's body for AFM and then reconsider. The test required a lumbar puncture, which had been done previously; and the sample was enough, so a second lumbar puncture wasn't necessary. A few hours later, the results of the test came back negative.

The coroner kept his word and signed off on Rylee's organ donation. It gave back some air to me and Kyle—not much, but enough to hang on to for the moment.

Continuing to work in twenty-four-hour shifts, members of the transplant bank began coordinating the transplant teams. Each organ Rylee donated had its own team that would remove the organ and transfer it into the recipient. We didn't know where these teams were coming from or where Rylee's organs were going, but we were aware that flights into Boise had to be coordinated.

WE HAD ARRIVED AT the hospital in Burns on October 29, and Rylee had been declared brain-dead in Boise on November 2. At 4:00 a.m. on November 4, Rylee was scheduled to give her gifts. We spent the early hours of that morning with her and our family so everyone could have a chance to say goodbye.

The transplant bank had given us heart necklaces for our family, and the hospital staff had taken footprints and handprints for mementos. Our moms took photos of Rylee's fingers placed around one of their fingers. During an ultrasound, we were able to sneak a recording of her heart, the sound of it beating strong and clear.

Kyle and I spent the last thirty minutes before the scheduled surgery alone with Rylee. The nurses arranged the room so we could sit in a chair and hold her one last time. I felt her warm little body in my arms and told her how much we loved her, how we always would, and how she was perfect and everything to us.

As Kyle sat in the chair and held Rylee, he looked down at her and said, "You'll have a dad in heaven. Joe will take care of you and love you up there. You won't be alone."

Those few words, spoken with love and tears, held more meaning to me than anything else I had ever heard. Of course Joe would take care of Rylee as if she were his own, just as Kyle had become a dad to Cody and Wade. I found comfort in that thought. Before that moment, I had felt like I was abandoning Rylee. Even though she was going to heaven, the idea of her being alone, without a parent to love her the way every baby deserves, was hard for me to face. Being a Christian, maybe I should have felt that the love of God and Jesus would be enough, but it wasn't. I wanted Rylee to have more, and I hated that I couldn't give it to her. So when Kyle said that Joe would be with her, tears of relief filled my eyes. I pictured Joe holding Rylee against his chest as he and my cousin Brittany looked down at her. They would take care of her. Heaven was already full of people who loved Rylee.

When 4:00 a.m. came, much too soon, the transplant teams came for Rylee. We followed as they wheeled her bed down the corridor, traveling slowly out of the PICU and into the quiet and seemingly empty halls of the children's hospital. But as we rounded the last corner, we realized the halls were, in fact, not empty.

Rylee was given a walk of honor. Every available doctor, nurse, and administrator in the hospital lined the walls and stood at attention. We walked between them, overwhelmed but feeling their love for our little girl. There were sad smiles and tears. Some staff members blew bubbles from wands as we walked by, adding a touch of lightness to the grave situation. In that way, they added something to the moment that Rylee would have enjoyed. Feeling that support, and knowing that others would remember this day and our daughter, was more valuable than any words or gifts could be.

When Kyle and I arrived at the elevator, it quickly filled with Rylee's bed, nurses, and doctors. We were given a few moments to say goodbye and give one last kiss on her smooth, warm forehead. Then we rode with her down the elevator to the operating floor; and as the doctors and nurses pushed Rylee's bed across the red line on the floor, we held hands and cried. That marked the end of our time with our daughter, the last time we would see her on this earth.

There was nothing else we could do. The family who remained at the hospital with us had gathered all our belongings. Together we walked out to our cars, silent in the eerie quiet of a city not yet awake. We hugged each other and then headed home.

As Kyle and I went back to Burns, I felt emptier than I thought possible. Driving those three hours away from Rylee was the hardest thing I had ever done. Even thinking about it today pulls the breath from my lungs and puts a weight on my chest. No one should have to drive home without their baby daughter, an empty carseat in the back.

Of course, it wouldn't be the hardest thing for long. How do you tell your children that their baby sister, someone they loved with everything they had, is dead? Once we got home, we called Joe's brother and his wife. They brought Cody and Wade to the house and quietly left to give us privacy.

The boys noticed right away that Rylee wasn't there. The first words out of their mouths were, "Where is Rylee? How is she doing?" Kyle and I gathered one son each on our laps, held them tight in our arms, and told them the simplified version: Rylee had gotten really sick, and while we and the doctors had tried as hard as we could, no one had been able to save her. Then we told them bluntly that Rylee had died and wasn't coming back. She was in heaven with their other dad. It was important for us to be straightforward about it. We didn't want to confuse the boys or make them think she was coming home. Then we sat next to each other on that couch, with the boys' arms wrapped around our necks and tears soaking our shirts, and hung on for dear life to what was left of our family.

20

L ATER THAT NIGHT, KYLE AND I posted the news on Facebook. While we hadn't given specifics about our situation, we had invited the community into our private lives when we asked for their prayers for Rylee. Thousands of prayers had been offered for Rylee—and for our family—around the community and from across the world. Our pastor had also led a prayer vigil for Rylee in Burns, where family, friends, and strangers gathered to support us.

Because of this response, Kyle and I felt it was important to share more about what had happened. It was difficult, since we still didn't really know how Rylee had died. What we did know, though, was the doctors and nurses in both Burns and Boise had done everything in their power to help us. The care we had received at both hospitals was amazing, and we wanted people in our community to know that. We didn't want people to question it. More importantly, we wanted the hospital staff, especially in Burns, to not blame themselves and to know we didn't blame them either.

We also felt it was important to share that Rylee was an organ donor. The ability for her to donate part of herself, to give life to others, was a blessing. It also gave us a gift we hadn't known was possible. This didn't justify her death; nothing would ever do that. But it gave us knowledge that something good had come out of our loss and that Rylee would be able to save other lives. It was a feeling, much like grief, that you have to experience in order to understand it.

We were given space to grieve as a family, but the community support was still clear. People in the area offered to help in whatever ways they could. A large group of friends and coworkers stacked and cut firewood for us. Others brought us food and took the boys out to play. These were people who had learned that, no matter how they helped, actively helping was better than just offering.

When Joe had died, Cody was a few weeks shy of turning three. At that point, he was too little to be around the amount of grief and pain that occurred at Joe's memorial service, so I let him come afterward for the potluck. For Rylee's service, however, Kyle and I knew it would be different. Cody and Wade needed to be there. They needed to see how much people loved her and have a chance to say goodbye in their own way.

Kyle and I agreed that we didn't want the service to focus on the loss or have an atmosphere steeped in sadness. We didn't think that would be healthy for the boys or representative of Rylee's personality. She had been filled with happiness, laughter, and smiles. We wanted her service to be a true celebration of life, so we let her brothers plan most of the ceremony.

We explained to Cody and Wade that we were going to have a party to celebrate Rylee and her life and the whole community would be invited. Then we asked the boys how they wanted to celebrate their sister, including the decorations they wanted and activities they thought Rylee would have loved.

The boys requested balloons—hundreds of them. Some would be filled with helium, and others wouldn't. Some would have pictures of PAW Patrol characters and Spider-Man, things the boys had planned to share with Rylee; and others would have images of things they thought she would have liked, such as unicorns and Care Bears. They wanted the party to be colorful, so we bought tablecloths in bright pinks, oranges, and blues, and scattered pink daisies on them. The boys also asked for cupcakes with pink, purple, and yellow frosting with a capital *R* on top of each; and a chocolate cake with purple and blue frosting and yellow and orange flowers. It was a challenge for the baker, but one she accepted. After all, she was one of Wade's preschool teachers, and she was more than happy to give him and his brother exactly what they wanted.

Cody and Wade also wanted pictures of Rylee everywhere. So a friend called some photography connections, and we received a large picture of Rylee and a blown-up copy of the family photo taken at Kyle's brother's wedding just over a month earlier. We reprinted pictures of all sizes that showed Rylee with her brothers, grandparents, me, and Kyle. Then we placed them around the room and strung them up on each wall. We also gathered her favorite stuffed animals and blankets and put them around the hall.

In addition, Cody and Wade wanted people to not just sign a guest book, but also make cards and draw pictures for Rylee. So we created an area where people could create something for our daughter. We covered a few tables with butcher paper and bought some paint and paintbrushes, and Cody asked the library if we could borrow other supplies from their craft room. By the end of Rylee's service, dozens of cards and pictures were scattered around the hall, all made by other children and people who loved her. They also wrote heartfelt notes to be buried with Rylee or for the four of us.

Still, the boys felt something was missing. So they asked for a bounce house. Yes, we had a bounce house for our beautiful daughter's celebration of life. It was a weird, unique, and perfect event.

For our family, Rylee's funeral was our fourth in less than four years. In many ways, it felt like we were becoming good at burying the people we loved. There were a lot of tears and hugs, but also a lot of laughter as we shared memories of all those we had lost. Our families loved the idea of a celebratory memorial, since it would allow the kids to honor Rylee in a way they understood more than the traditional mourning of a memorial service.

Hundreds of people from throughout the community came for Rylee's celebration of life. We knew some of them well, but others were strangers or acquaintances. Some brought their children, who played, laughed, and hugged Cody and Wade, offering them a pure and innocent form of support.

Our pastor—the same man who had married me and Joe, buried Joe, married me and Kyle, and baptized Kyle—spoke at Rylee's celebration of life. The man whose church we attended most Sundays, who taught us about God and had seen so much happen in my life, was there that day, and he talked about love, loss, and heaven. Kyle and I also spoke, mainly about Rylee and how she was a blessing and a courageous miracle. And our pastor's wife performed a perfect rendition of the song "Bedtime Prayer" on the piano. Tears glistened in her eyes as she sang and streamed down the cheeks of many of the people in attendance. Yes, Rylee's celebration of life was filled with sadness. But more importantly, it was filled with love, hope, light, and life. We had lost our daughter, but in that room and at that moment, there was no room for darkness.

The next day, Rylee was buried next to Joe at the ranch. Joe's brother, dad, and grandfather gave us permission to do this—in fact, they told us we didn't even need to ask. Rylee was family and should be buried with family. It was a small comfort to know she wasn't alone in a different cemetery and surrounded by strangers.

Rylee was buried in a tiny white casket that was covered in flowers. She wore a dress made by a woman in our community using the lace wedding dress I had worn for my and Kyle's wedding. Inside her casket, she was covered by the blue-and-white blanket from Dr. D's sister and surrounded with pictures of her family, notes and letters, and the inner heart of the necklaces that the transplant bank had given us and our family.

Once again, our pastor spoke about love, loss, and heaven to the large group of family and friends who had gathered at the ranch. His wife sang another lullaby, "All the Pretty Little Ponies"; and I cried silently as the casket was lowered by Rylee's uncles into the ground.

Today, Rylee's headstone stands tall next to Joe's. It's covered in carvings: roses on the sides, her name on the front, and the words Courageous Miracle on the back, with butterflies fluttering toward heaven.

21

A FEW WEEKS AFTER RYLEE's burial, we received a call from the doctor who had first seen Rylee at the children's hospital in Boise. The results for Rylee's botulism test had come back—and it was positive.

I had forgotten about that test. Kyle and I had already accepted that we'd never know what had happened to Rylee. After all, doctors, an autopsy, and DNA testing had never been able to tell us why Joe had died, so I had let go of any hope for answers. Learning the results, though, was like a punch in the gut. We still wouldn't know why Rylee had gone into cardiac arrest or why the doctors hadn't been able to save her. We had done our best to focus on her short but amazing life and the miracles she had given other people. But with this phone call, I was forced to go back to that dark place. It was shocking and frustrating, because it didn't make any difference. The knowledge couldn't save her. The reason no longer mattered. Rylee was still gone.

Before that call, all I knew about infant botulism was that babies could get it from eating honey. That's why doctors tell you never to feed it to a baby for the first few years of their life. I had followed that rule, though. So what happened? The Centers for Disease Control and Prevention (CDC) called me and Kyle for an interview, since botulism is very dangerous and the CDC closely monitors such cases to ensure they're not a result of biological terrorism. However, it was determined that Rylee's case was not associated with that or with contamination of her formula or other products she was using.

After this, I contacted the Infant Botulism Treatment and Prevention Program (IBTPP) in California, the national experts on infant botulism. We learned from them that botulism naturally occurs when a baby ingests the spores created by the bacterium *Clostridium botulinum*. These spores then colonize, growing within the baby's large intestine and producing a neurotoxin. While the spores are often found in honey, research had found that infant botulism is most commonly due to swallowing microscopic dust particles that can carry the spores. We hadn't fed Rylee honey, but she could have ingested the spores from breathing in dust at our house, during a trip to the ranch, or from the fruits and vegetables we brought home from the store.

While researching infant botulism, I found that while the disease is very serious, it's also very rare, with only 130 to 150 cases in the US each year. In other words, approximately 3.5 to 4 babies out of every 100,000 born in the US, or 0.0035 percent, contract infant botulism. The medical community doesn't have much understanding of this disease. Nor do they know why some babies are susceptible to it while many others aren't. Typically, when an infant contracts infant botulism, doctors have enough time to diagnose and treat it. Recovery is typically slow; the affected children require months in critical care units and often have lingering effects. We didn't have that time with Rylee, however. For some reason, she was more susceptible to it. According to the IBTPP, Rylee's case was only the fourth confirmed death of infant botulism in the US in the last twenty years. Researchers think it may be likely that other deaths from infant botulism have occurred, possibly in cases of Sudden Infant Death Syndrome, but the disease's rarity makes it difficult to study or to confirm such cases.

After that call with the IBTPP, Kyle and I each found ways to take the blame on ourselves. It's human nature to blame; and since we couldn't blame each other, we each tried to blame ourselves. But the more we talked, the more we reminded each other that we didn't know where the spores had come from, that Rylee had exhibited symptoms of a cold and we had taken care of her based on what we knew. We walked ourselves through a million different scenarios to prove to ourselves, and each other, that we did everything we could have for our little girl.

That was our only answer. God only knows why Rylee was so susceptible to the botulism and we didn't even have time to diagnose her. Only He knows why this all happened, and I guarantee you that when I get to heaven, there will be an inquisition. But at that moment, I had to accept that Rylee had died, even though the fact that it happened was (and still is) really, really shitty.

But I chose not to focus on the loss, or the knowledge that Rylee was one of a tiny fraction of babies to get infant botulism and an even tinier fraction to die from it. Instead, I concentrated on the fact that we had had Rylee, even for a short time. She had been happy and loved. While I would have given almost anything to have saved her, I couldn't let the loss let me forget that she had lived. And if I too wanted to live and not get lost in the darkness, then that was what I had to focus on: the fact that Rylee had lived.

At the same time, it was a relief to finally have some answers. Infant botulism occurs when the spores are digested and produce toxins in the baby's immature digestive tract. Once the digestive tract is more mature, generally when a baby is around twelve months old, the spores tend to pass through the body without producing any toxin. I no longer had to spend the night checking on the boys, waiting for the time I would walk in their room to find them dead from some unknown cause. Now I knew that what had killed Rylee wouldn't come after Cody and Wade too.

22

W HEN I WAS EIGHTEEN YEARS old, I got a tattoo. It was a way for me to prove I was an adult, even though I was just a senior in high school. I went with my two best friends, who watched in admiration (they were still only seventeen) as I got a small tattoo of the Chinese character 希, which means "hope." I looked it up and brought it in to the artist just to make sure it was right. I loved the design and the meaning; to the eighteen-year-old me, it just felt right. Little did I know how much I would need hope in the future.

Following my second miscarriage, with depression and insomnia wearing on me and grief heavy on my heart, I knew I had to do something. I was able to sleep, but my soul hadn't healed. While I was still able to love Joe and Cody, my heart was still shattered, and each step I took scattered the pieces even more. I needed something that would help me start piecing my heart back together.

Around Christmas of 2013, I knew what I wanted to do. And I knew it would help because, once I had decided it, I finally felt calm in my soul for the first time since our second miscarriage.

At that time, I had one living child (Cody) and three who hadn't survived. Those three babies had only existed for me and Joe, but they had existed. I didn't want to forget them or move on and keep it quiet as I felt society dictated. After all, if miscarriage was a socially acceptable subject to talk about, why hadn't I known how many people in my life had also experienced a miscarriage before I had mine? I needed something to document these children I had carried, to serve as a reminder of them and make them real. A memorial of some kind to represent not my failure, but their existence and the fact that they were loved and would always be missed.

So I convinced Joe that I needed another tattoo, something permanent I could carry with me always and never lose. Despite the fact that Joe didn't like tattoos and already considered the two I had to be two too many, he didn't question me. He loved me and wanted to help me feel better, and he supported anything and everything that I told him I needed. It turned out that, despite my attempt to hide my depression, he knew I was going through it; and he tried to give me space and be there when I reached out.

I had never been artistic. But Joe was good at designing, a skill he had honed through his work as an engineer. So I described what I wanted: three broken hearts (though I didn't want it to be too obvious that they were hearts), with three flowers of different colors, one for each of the little humans we had created and lost. Joe sketched the image in pencil on engineering paper, then sat with me as I got it tattooed on my ankle. It was a place on my body that I could hide or display as I wanted and could see and touch to know that the babies and the loss were real.

In July 2016, a little over a year after Joe had passed, Kyle took me to Boise to get a memorial tattoo for Joe. By then, the sharpness of my memories with Joe had begun to blur, and I had started to forget the sound of his voice. So I decided I needed tangible things besides the widow's ring and the necklace I'd had made with Joe's wedding band to remind me and others that Joe was real.

Kyle had introduced me to a tattoo parlor in Boise that employed some of the best tattoo artists I had ever seen. He had been to the shop before, to get a memorial tattoo for his dad. After looking at the artist portfolios online, I decided which artist's work I liked the most and made an appointment. Then Kyle listened while I bounced ideas for my memorial tattoo of Joe off him. In the end, I decided on a monochrome daisy surrounded by feathery filigree. It resembled a leather design Joe had planned to put on a pair of spur straps for me. I had it tattooed between my shoulder blades as Kyle watched from across the room.

So after Rylee died, I wanted to honor her as well. I wanted to carry her with me always, and I wanted tangible items I could use to remember her. Once again, people in our community stepped up to help us. One neighbor made teddy bears out of Rylee's pajamas. On Cody and Wade's bears, she created pockets that each held a picture of Rylee and embroidered the words My Shooting Star (Cody's nickname for Rylee) on the back. Another friend made for us a blanket out of Rylee's clothes. And I had a ring, a white gold band with a simple inset purple stone and etched with the name Rylee Marie, made for my right ring finger.

As with Joe, I wanted to document her life and our loss on my body. Even as Kyle and I sat in the children's hospital, knowing we would lose Rylee, we talked about getting memorial tattoos for her. We told her how we'd carry her with us in hearts full of love, heads full of memories, and tattoos on our bodies. We both knew how tattoos were cathartic and healing for us, so we spent hours talking about what would represent Rylee best. By the time we left, we only knew we wanted purple butterflies and flowers.

Kyle and I went back to the same tattoo artist who had done my tattoo for Joe. We told him we wanted memorial tattoos to represent our beautiful daughter. We didn't know what we wanted specifically besides purple butterflies and flowers, but that was why we went to someone who was truly an artist. The tattoo artist came up with two different designs, one for each of us. On Kyle's left arm, he embedded flowers and butterflies that were as bold and masculine as they could be, with tiny details scratched into the butterflies' wings.

For me, the tattoo artist designed cherry blossoms, realistic in grayscale, that wrapped around a beautiful three-dimensional butterfly that appeared to have landed gently on my shoulder. Then I chose one more, one that the world would be able to see unless I wore a long-sleeved shirt. On my left forearm, the artist tattooed the words Courageous Miracle in beautiful black script he designed just for me.

Today, I carry both tattoos with pride. Each person who sees them, even if they don't ask about the meaning behind them, is able to see a little piece of Rylee. These tattoos are marks of my grief. As much as I may feel that I'm grieving well, there is no getting over any loss; and the loss of a child is so much harder, because it was my job to keep her safe and I failed. Not a day goes by that I don't apologize to Rylee. But I'll never be able to apologize enough to make it better. It will never be OK that she died and we lost her. Still, I'll continue to apologize and remember.

I'm so sorry, Rylee. I'm so sorry, little girl.

23

EVERY DAY I WAKE UP, and the pain of losing Rylee is still there. I can still feel the cold of the shock. Sometimes the hurt causes me to gasp for breath. Other times, the hurt causes tears to stream suddenly from my eyes. Often I carry the hurt close to me, in my heart, where I feel it but others can't see it. To anyone who looks at me, I may seem recovered. But there is no recovering from grief, and there is no going back. There is only going forward as I bear my grief.

As I continue with my life, grief isn't the only emotion I carry. Losing Joe and Rylee has planted in me a constant fear that the people I love can be taken from me and I can do nothing to stop it. This fear will hit me at the most random times. I've felt it at night, when I wake in the dark and fear Kyle has stopped breathing; or at the park while Cody and Wade are playing, where I imagine them falling, hitting their head, and dying right before my eyes. In those moments, I have to stop myself from grabbing them and never letting them go.

But what kind of a life would that be for them? Or for me?

Through loss, I've learned that fear is real. But I've also learned that it doesn't need to control my life. Ignoring the fear doesn't make it go away. Pretending that I don't feel it allows it to keep festering, just under the surface, so it can erupt in sudden panic or anxiety attacks. So I've learned not to ignore it, but to recognize it. Doing so takes away the power it holds over me. I recognize that what I fear could happen; then I consider the likelihood of it coming true. If the fear is legitimate and I determine that something bad is likely to happen, I allow myself to take reasonable action to prevent it from happening. But when it's not a legitimate fear, that's much harder for me. After all, what was the likelihood of Joe literally dropping dead at the age of thirty? Or of Brittany dying from complications due to a rare and unknown tumor? Or Rylee succumbing to infant botulism?

My life has been filled with unlikely events. Sometimes I feel I'm cursed, that my life will continue to be filled with things that aren't likely to happen. And yet logic tells me that, statistically, all the terrible things I fear shouldn't happen. So that's what I grab onto. Despite my past, I grab onto the hope that the odds will be with me. I grab onto the belief that whatever I'm fearful about shouldn't—and probably won't—happen.

After I've recognized my fear and looked at the chances of that fear coming true, I say one simple word, usually in my head, that allows me to confront that fear.

No.

No, I won't act unreasonably.

No, I won't place my fears on the people I love.

No, I won't let fear make my decisions for me.

Just no.

Even if this exercise doesn't completely shut the fear down, it at least pushes the fear down enough so that the fear doesn't control me. It reins in the fear enough to prevent me from telling my kids they can't play on the slide because it's too dangerous. It lets me be in charge and makes my life livable, survivable.

Even when Kyle and I were in the hospital with Rylee, I knew I would survive this loss. I had no idea how, and I'm still not sure how I've survived this long. But I know that sharing the weight of this grief with others has helped.

I've grown from the darkness and come out of it stronger than when I first went in after losing Joe. And with each loss I've been forced to face, I've become stronger—not because I don't grieve, but because I've developed the confidence to find a way to piece myself back together. I'm confident that I won't just survive, but rather live my life to the fullest, since I know too well how short life can be. The marks of grief on my soul will heal like the gold and silver lines on a kintsugi vase, and I'll be stronger because of all I've gone through.

IN ADDITION TO FINDING the strength and confidence I felt I had lost when Joe died, I found something else I didn't know I needed: my voice.

When I lost Joe, I shared only what I felt I needed to share. I would answer questions about losing Joe, but I wouldn't volunteer information. When Kyle and I lost Rylee, though, we were more open about our experience. In the months that followed, I was amazed at the number of people who thanked me not just because we satisfied their curiosity or let them in, but also because we helped them in some way by sharing our and Rylee's story.

By talking about my losses, I realized I could help other people while reminding myself that I wasn't alone. The more I talked about loss and owned my feelings, the more the weight of each loss would lift away. It became easier to breathe with my grief. And if I could help others by sharing my story, that was even better. Helping just one person gave some meaning to the loss, and it wouldn't happen unless I opened myself up.

I have my story, but other people have their stories too. And the grief is so much lighter when we share our stories with each other.

Losing Rylee opened my and Kyle's eyes to organ donation. This is one small part of the story, but it has had such an effect on us. Most people know that organ donation can save lives, but we wanted to share our story and promote organ donation on the basis that while it does save lives, which is amazing in itself, it can also help to heal broken hearts and shattered souls. Organ donation affects and benefits more than the people who receive the organs. In a way, it saved me and Kyle too.

The people we wanted to share our story with most were the recipients of Rylee's organs and their families. Sometimes when people receive an organ transplant, they feel guilty that someone else died so that their life could be saved. Kyle and I didn't know if any of the recipients of Rylee's organs felt this way, but we wanted to let them know we didn't see it that way. From our perspective, our daughter didn't die so someone else could live. Rather, she died, and then she saved the recipients of her organs. Rylee's death wasn't caused by their need. Her ability to save three lives and give hope and happiness to who knows how many others was a gift to us. We wanted to thank the recipients and their families for that gift, and we wanted to share a little bit of Rylee with them.

Through the transplant bank, Kyle and I were allowed to write anonymous letters and send pictures to the recipients using strict guidelines to ensure no privacy violations occurred. Any response from the recipients would be completely voluntary; they may not even choose to look at the letters. But we wanted to write to the recipients anyway. We wanted to write them for ourselves. A few months later, we received a letter from the transplant bank. They informed us that all three transplants had taken place. A baby boy had received Rylee's heart, a little girl her liver, and a diabetic woman her kidneys. Rylee had gifted three people more time in this world. That knowledge alone took away a little more weight from my grief.

Currently, Kyle and I have heard back from the recipient of Rylee's kidneys via the transplant bank. The letter, which was written on stationery featuring a shooting star, brought us sadness, happiness, smiles, and tears. We will continue to correspond anonymously, though if the recipients request to contact us directly, we would be honored to meet with them in person. In fact, I hope that will happen. I want to know the other, happier half of the story. Kyle and I know the sad part. I want to talk to and hug the people who live with Rylee's organs. More importantly, Kyle and I want them to know firsthand how much the opportunity to donate her organs has helped heal our family. I pray for the recipients daily and hope her gifts were the miracles they needed. Even in our darkest hours, hope still exists, and this entire process has shown us that.

Kyle and I will continue to share our and Rylee's story however we can. Rylee's face is one of many on a quilt that was made in honor of donors and recipients from 2018. I spoke at the quilt's unveiling and also at the 2019 OHSU transplant picnic, an event with hundreds of organ recipients in attendance. I told them that their survival means something to the donor's families, regardless of whether they contact each other, and that they are gifts to others as well. We will continue to share our story, because by helping each person who hears it, we strengthen Rylee's legacy. It's a legacy that's already larger than many of us can hope for, since Rylee saved three lives in the less than four months she lived. I like to think that sharing her story helps others. At the few events where Kyle and I have spoken, a few attendees approached us afterward and told us they had never wanted to contact their donor's families out of fear that it would be too hard for them. But after hearing our story, they were moved to try to connect with those families. Maybe it was part of the grand scheme of things, but I hope that hearing our story made a difference for someone.

So Kyle and I will share. And we will heal. And we will grow. We'll try not to take life or love for granted because, as bad as it's been, we know it could be worse. Even as we grieved for Rylee, we watched news stories showing entire families lost in the California wildfires. We heard horror stories of suffering, and I can't imagine what those people went through. Life is something to be cherished and embraced, even though it can be so hard, so sad, and so tiring.

IT'S INTERESTING HOW GRIEF works. It's hard and exhausting, and much of the time it's not rational. When Rylee was a few weeks old, Kyle and I realized she got extra gassy after I drank milk or ate cheese. Since I was breastfeeding her, I went off the dairy products. This was hard for me, since I regularly drank about a gallon or more of milk a week, ate enough cheese to kill a mouse, and loved ice cream. But I gave up milk and tried to limit my sneaks to a small glass every few weeks when I was really craving it. Then Rylee would get gassy and uncomfortable after breastfeeding, and I would feel bad. Even though I was willing to cut back on dairy for her sake, just as I was willing to do anything else for her, I hated that I had to do it.

So when Rylee died, I could go back to eating all the dairy I wanted—and yet I couldn't bring myself to touch it. Slowly I added cheese and ice cream back into my diet, but for some reason the thought of drinking a nice cold glass of milk made me feel ill. There was no logical reason for this. Maybe I felt as if drinking milk was somehow a betrayal to Rylee. Maybe it was my way of proving I would still give up anything for her. Even now, after so much time has passed, I have a glass of milk only on occasion, and it lacks the enjoyment I used to get from it.

I've also avoided honey in a similar but stronger way. I was never a huge lover of honey, but something about a honey and peanut butter sandwich on a summer afternoon is refreshing . . . especially with a tall glass of ice-cold milk. I also used to love dipping pizza crust into warm honey. Kyle and I didn't feed Rylee any honey, and we rarely used the honey we kept in the cupboard. Still, the knowledge that honey can lead to infant botulism, that the spores could have somehow been transferred from one of us to her, even though that risk is small, was too much. So we threw away the honey in the cupboard. A few weeks after Rylee passed, a new bottle we had ordered arrived in the mail. So far, it remains unopened and tucked away, a symbol of the irrational choices grief can cause us to make.

.

24

EVERY YEAR AFTER THE FIRST branding I attended when Joe and I were dating, I was given increasingly important tasks such as giving shots or keeping records. Eventually it was my responsibility to cook, preparing cinnamon rolls and coffee for everyone in the mornings and a good, hearty meal in the afternoon. Once Cody was born, we ensured Cody experienced the brandings and learned about his heritage. I would make the trip between the house and the corrals countless times during the day, checking on food and helping however I could.

But when it was time for the first branding after Joe's death, I couldn't bring myself to do the work. Joe's dad and grandpa asked a neighbor to prepare the meal. I tried to help, but my state of mind made it too difficult.

I wasn't sure where I belonged anymore. I needed to be there, at the ranch, and so did the boys. Branding cows was part of their heritage. Yet my grief had stripped me of my role in the brandings. I didn't belong in the house, making dinner. Nor did I belong in the branding trap, cheering Joe on.

It was impossible to witness the branding and not see Joe's face in the crowd. As I watched from the side of the branding pen, I felt sympathy for the calves. The conversation I had had with Joe the evening after our first branding together came back to me, especially the part about how the branding makes the calves less carefree and marks the time when they're forced to grow up. In that way, I could relate to the calves. Joe's death marked the line between my old, innocent life and my life of loss. It was a mark of pain on the soul, distinguishing the before and the after. At that time, I didn't know how I would survive or what I would become. Much like those freshly branded calves, I felt raw and hurt by my experience. I knew I would survive, but I was forever changed. However, unlike those calves, no one could see how I was marked by that loss.

Now, years after losing Joe, I can take up my old role again. I can step back into the kitchen and feed the people who come to our brandings. I can go to the branding trap and watch with the sadness and warmth of Joe's memory. I can see the calves and find comfort in knowing they'll survive the pain, just as I have survived. Those calves will forever be marked by their brands, just as I'm marked by the tattoos I put on my body to memorialize my losses. The scars will be with me for the rest of my life. I'll wear them proudly, but I won't let them define me.

Other firsts after Joe's death were hard as well, such as the first wedding I attended alone, the first anniversary, the first birthday, and the first day of school. Some of the seconds were hard too, and even some of the thirds and fourths. All days, not just the milestone events, can be tough. No one gets a break from grief. Life is hard when you live with it. Even happy moments have an underlying sadness. That's just how life is now. We have to remember and bear the sadness, pain, and grief because of how much we love, and the love is the important part.

Pain isn't always a part of love, though, especially for Cody and Wade. They were small when Joe died. Wade, of course, has no memories of Joe except for what we give him through stories and photographs. He didn't grieve for Joe, but in the future, as he gets older, he may find his own grief for him. Cody, who was almost three years old when Joe died, does remember Joe, but not very much. He'll experience glimpses here and there or say things that aren't part of stories or photographs. But Cody never really cried for Joe. It was as if he knew his dad was gone and understood it. He never asked for Joe after he died, like many kids will ask for their parents. In fact, Cody's original grief was very matter-of-fact. He would see something that had been Joe's or a place Joe had taken him, and he would look at me and say in a quiet, solemn, and unemotional voice, "That was my dad's, but he's dead, so now it's yours."

Cody and Wade grieved for Rylee much more, though, and in different ways. Wade, for example, grieves in outbursts of crying. He'll suddenly erupt into heart-wrenching sounds, tears streaming down his face. Often it happens when he's playing. When we ask him what's wrong, he'll wail that he misses his sister. Wade's grief comes suddenly but its acuteness is over once he lets it out. Then, after we hold him for a few minutes and tell him we miss her too, he goes back to playing.

Cody's grief for Rylee flares up when he's exhausted. But his grief for her, and possibly for Joe, has evolved. In some ways, his grief is much like mine for Joe, stripping him of confidence. Simple things such as telling Cody to put on his shoes with a note of impatience in my voice can send him to a place of feeling worthless; he'll question if he deserves me, Kyle, Wade, the house we live in, and just about anything. Sometimes he'll get into trouble after making a choice that millions of other young boys have made; and when Kyle and I talk to him about it, he'll say he feels like he deserves to be in more trouble and then hit himself on the head or bend back his fingers, trying to hurt himself. Sometimes his grief is so strong that he wishes he would just die so he could see Rylee in heaven.

As a parent, my children's grief kills me. It's so much harder to face than my own grief, which was hard enough. When Cody first said he wanted to die, my initial reaction was, "Don't talk like that." Later, Kyle and I realized that wasn't the right response. If Cody is feeling that way, he needs to talk about it. He needs to feel like he has a safe place to share those feelings, and we need to be that safe place for him. So we encourage him to talk about his feelings. It doesn't matter if it's with us, a teacher, a grandparent, or a pediatric therapist.

I am not my boys, though. I don't know the form of their grief or how it will change as they grow older. Many times, I don't know if I'm making the right choices. Kyle and I can spend hours discussing what we should do, yet I'll still fear, as I have since Joe died, that I'll mess up my boys even more. They have experienced so much grief and not enough innocence in their lives so far. It's hard to remember that should-have-beens can kill you. We have to focus on how to help our sons as much as possible. So we take each day in stride as best we can. Sometimes I make mistakes and bad decisions. But there's one thing I always have confidence in: I love my boys unconditionally, and I make sure they know it. In fact, I tell them so often that Cody regularly responds, "I know. You tell me all the time."

I had already known loss, trauma, and grief before Rylee passed. So when she died, I went through the grieving process as I knew I would. I knew the darkness, tears, fog, and tiredness would come. Kyle knew what his grief would look like too. So we talked about it. We prepared and made sure we had time to go boldly into the darkness when our souls needed it. I knew I would find growth in the darkness and then peace once I escaped. I imagined my once-again shattered soul being restored, this time with streaks of purple. And I knew I would survive and would choose to be a better person than I was before.

During that process, I discovered my grief for Rylee is no less than that for Joe, yet very different. And while that grief is just as strong, my ability to carry it has improved, and its weight was lightened by Kyle's presence. With Joe, I was in that grief alone. I was the only wife, the only one who had lost a husband. No one else, no matter how much they grieved for Joe, had the same experiences in their grief. With Rylee, I grieved for her in my own way, following my body's process, but I didn't do it alone. Kyle lost a daughter too, and grieved for her. I guess the cliché that misery loves company is true—not because it makes us happy to know others are going through it, but because when others go through the same grief with us, they're in the darkness with you. And there's comfort in knowing you're not there alone. On some level, someone understands how you feel, even if how they deal with grief is worlds away from how you deal with yours. Between Kyle's presence, my coach's teachings, and other things I learned on my own, I was able to take back some power from the darkness even though my grief for Rylee was just as strong as it was for Joe.

THROUGHOUT MY LIFE, I'VE seen one truth over and over again: we grieve because we love. Grief doesn't exist without love, and love encompasses both unimaginable joy and horrific grief. Every time we open up our hearts to love, we accept the risk of grief— and it's a big risk. Everything that is living will die. But there's a difference between the death of someone you love and the death of love. Love doesn't die. You can see it every time the memory of someone you've lost makes you smile. Joe's mom taught me that there's always room for more love, and more love is never something to fear.

It can be hard to smile at the memories, especially when the loss is so fresh or acute. And it's easy to let the darkness pull you down and take over. I always feared the darkness until I realized it wasn't the darkness itself I feared. Rather, I was afraid I would never escape it—that I would be alone, miserable, scared, and stuck where there was no hope. Now I know there's a way out of the darkness, but I have to take it upon myself to climb out.

The times I stayed in the darkness the longest were the times when I would see or hear something that I knew I should smile or laugh at. But instead of giving myself permission to smile or laugh, I would turn my head and choose to believe my life was miserable and I didn't deserve to enjoy it when the people I loved were dead. It has been a long journey, and I now realize that those little things are my sources of hope: laughter, smiles, and hugs from a child; a beautiful sunrise; a puppy; a thunderstorm over the desert. They are the little glimmer of light, sneaking into the darkness. Sometimes they're bright, other times faint, but they always penetrate the darkness. It's my responsibility, my choice, to embrace them. I have to choose to grab onto the light, the hope, and let it pull me out of the darkness. I have to choose that living after loss is OK. Smiling, laughing, living, loving—it's all ok, but it also has to be a choice.

Grieving is hard work. You don't get to choose if someone lives or dies, but you do get to choose how to live with your grief. Will you let it keep you in the darkness and fill you with sadness? Or will you find your way out? Choosing the latter is different than never going into the darkness and never being sad. You *will* be sad—horribly, immensely sad in a way that's beyond words. But that's OK. Someone you loved has died; it's OK to be sad about it. Where the choice comes in is if you decide you'll let that loss define the rest of your life. Will you let the loss overpower your memories of the past and choke out any happiness for the future? Or will you embrace your sadness—recognize it, name it, accept it—and then introduce it to happiness? The two emotions aren't mutually exclusive. Your happiness, no matter where it comes from, can live side by side with your sadness over your loss, just like your love for one person can live side by side with your love for another.

No matter how long ago your loss happened, things will trigger your sadness over it. You may have heard how the big firsts are so hard, like birthdays, holidays, and graduations. But the seconds, thirds, and every milestone after are also hard. The trigger could be a sunrise, a book, or even a moment. It can be filling out *single* on a form that doesn't offer *widow* as an option, or realizing time and again that you have no emergency contact. It can also be each time you need help getting kids dressed in the morning, or seeing a little girl who would be your daugther's age if your daughter was still alive. Grief is much more than the notable firsts. For those who experience it, they feel it every day and in every moment. Some moments will sting more than others, but the grief is always there.

Sometimes, all I can think of saying is, "It's so stupid that this is my life! It's so unfair!" And then I'm given a little light, and I correct myself. It isn't that I have a stupid, horrible, unfair life. Rather, stupid and horrible things have altered my life forever, and it's unfair that those events happened. For me, it's important to distinguish the difference. I need to remember that my life is so much more than the losses I've experienced, but it will only be what I make of it. I have a choice: to wallow in these shitty events, or to recognize what they are and know there's more to my life. I have to choose to make my life worth more, to continue to grab onto the light and pull myself out and live, even with my grief.

Grief doesn't leave. I must carry its weight with me forever. And so I'll continue to hesitate over a glass of milk, spurn honey, and stare creepily at Kyle and the boys while they sleep to make sure they're still breathing. In these and other ways, grief has changed me. It has stripped me of my innocence and my delusions that awful things only happen to other people. And as hard as it is to admit, grief has also changed me for the better. I now know that I can survive. I'm more resilient; and while I may not always want to survive the unimaginable, I can. There's power in knowing this, even though it's mixed with sadness. I can survive if something happens to Kyle or the boys. I'll survive the loss of others I love. Yes, I'm strong, but there's a sadness in no longer saying "I couldn't survive without you" or "I don't know what I'd do without you," because I do know. I would find a way to survive, and I would embrace all those moments that define life and memories. Yes, I will shatter, but I will heal with each loss, another colored lacquer holding me together.

I don't know how my story will end, though I have no doubt that I'll continue to love. I'm equally sure that I'll continue to lose the people I love. No one is safe from death, and grief is a darkness that will settle on everyone who risks their heart by loving. What I do know is my story will be one of a full and happy life that I choose despite the sadness that can grip it. I'll continue to have days where I'll struggle to live with the weight of my loss; and I'll rely on the light of Kyle, Cody, Wade, and others who love me to pull me through the darkness. And I'll continue to grow under the weight of the grief I'll always carry with me. I still have so much to learn about myself, my grief, and living my life; and I'll strive to continue learning about it until my last breath. Most importantly,

I'll hold onto hope. My Chinese-character tattoo is a constant reminder that hope is always around. I just have to choose to see it and remember where to find it.

My story isn't extraordinary. But it is mine, and I wouldn't change it for the world. I have no regrets. So I'll continue to live my life the best I can. And I hope that, through my story, you've been able to find your own strength and hope.

Autumn and Brittany, 1993

Autumn and Joe, 2006

Autumn and Joe, 2009

Joe and Brittany, 2010

Brittany, 2011

Grandpa Chuck and Cody, 2012

Autumn and Joe at Hoover Dam, 2013

Joe and Cody, 2014

Joe and Wade, 2015

Back of Joe's headstone, 2015

Autumn, Cody, and Wade, 2016

Autumn, Kyle, Cody, and Wade, 2017

Memorial table at Kyle and Autumn's wedding, 2017

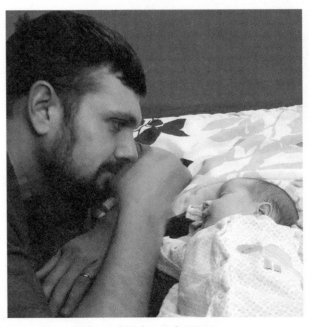

Kyle and Rylee, July 2018

Rylee, August 2018

Rylee, August 2018

Wade and Rylee, September 2018

Rylee, September 2018

Autumn, Kyle, Cody, Wade, and Rylee
at a wedding, September 2018

Cody and Rylee, October 2018

Autumn and Rylee, October 2018

Back of Rylee's Headstone, 2019

Joe and Rylee's headstones, 2019

Cemetery, 2019

Appendix

Lessons from Grief

I've learned a lot about my grief, and I hope I've passed many of those lessons on to you. Here are a few things that I learned. Not all these items will fit with your grief, but I hope you find some similarities with your experiences. Everyone deserves to know they're not alone.

1. Grief doesn't exist without love. Love is always worth the grief, but how grief is expressed isn't a measure of love. There is no way to measure love. Just because a person may seem to "get over" loss quickly doesn't mean they didn't love deeply. You can only see the grief they're willing to show. It's OK to show a lot or a little.

2. Grief is relative to what you have experienced in the past. I didn't know the extent of grief until I lived through it. If all you've lived through is the loss of a pet, that may be the worst pain you can imagine. Once you live through more loss, you realize that grief is not only complicated, but also different for each individual who has to shoulder that weight and even within yourself. My grief for Joe is very different than my grief for Brittany, Grandpa Chuck, or Rylee.

3.   Grief is individual. What you would do may not be the same thing that someone else who's grieving would do. Also, grief has no timeline. Everyone grieves at their own pace. Everyone has to do what they need to do. Judgment, even with the best of intentions, is more hurtful than helpful. Be your own judge.

4.   People will say stupid things. Most of these words aren't meant to hurt you. Rather, they're words of intended support spoken by people who don't know better. Try to have patience with these people. If you're supporting someone who is grieving, please remember that it never helps to rationalize their loss, even if what you say is true. Here are some true statements that are unlikely to provide comfort:
    a.   They're in a better place.
    b.   It's part of God's plan.
    c.   At least you're still young and can remarry / have more kids.
    d.   You're so strong.

5.   Shock is real. It's a physical or stress response to emotional pain. For me, shock shows itself through temperature. I was always cold and in an emotional fog. I also lost my appetite and even some of my hair. To this day, I have huge gaps in my memory from the periods when I was deepest in my grief. Some of the memories I do have only prove the intensity of the fog, like leaving the car running in the driveway after getting home or putting my keys in the freezer. Shock can last for hours, days, weeks, or even years. In some cases,

when the shock wears off is when the pain of grief is most acute and the darkness most overpowering.

6. No words will make someone feel better when they suffer trauma. No one understands your loss, and you can't understand anyone else's. You can't fully imagine it, so don't bother trying. Instead, simply say that you're sorry and then be there for that person.

7. Grief never goes away. It will change as you change, but it will always be present. You can fight grief, but you won't win. It's OK to be sad, cry, and show your grief. Don't apologize for it. The act of grieving provides healing. Embrace your grief when you can, even when it makes others uncomfortable. Go boldly into the darkness so you can find the light once again.

8. Trauma and grief change you on a visceral level. When they occur, your life divides into a before and an after. You can no longer be the person you were before. Instead, you have to choose the person you'll become. In the long run, you can choose to let grief destroy you or to rebuild a new you in spite of it.

9. Even years after your loss, acute grief can be triggered in a million different ways, either expected or unexpected. You can't hide from the triggers. You can either try to avoid your response or choose to embrace it. I try to embrace it: to feel my feelings, recognize them, and move forward anyway.

10. Grief isn't just mourning the loss of an individual. The loss you experience when someone you love dies is multilayered. Yes, you mourn the person, but you also mourn secondary things such as the future, laughter, routine, and even arguments.

11. The question *why* has no answers. Even if it can be answered a few times, another *why* always lies underneath. You can either dwell on it or figure out how to accept the fact that no answer will make it OK.

12. The idea of family is so much more than blood. The people who are part of your family are the people who love and support you unconditionally. Family can be your light in the darkness.

13. Grief is hard. Some people do it alone, but I couldn't. When people offer to help, accept it. If you need help, ask for it. Nothing is wrong with needing a hand. And when you offer help, don't leave it open-ended. Be specific in your offer (what you offer, when, where, etc.), and make it hard for the grieving peson to turn it down.

14. It's bittersweet to know you can survive the worst loss imaginable and to no longer tell the people you love that you couldn't live without them. In learning your own strength and ability to survive, you lose a certain amount of innocence.

15. There is some truth to the saying "Fake it until you

make it." By allowing myself to smile and laugh at things that my brain told me should make me react that way, I was able to convince my body that smiling and laughing were OK. Eventually I wasn't just plastering on fake smiles or forcing hollow laughs. I would feel the happiness as well.

16. Embrace life. Smile and laugh, even through the tears. Emotions aren't mutually exclusive. Being happy about something doesn't mean you aren't sad, angry, or frustrated.

17. Find someone who can talk you through grief and who you can open up to without fear of judgment. Talking can be hard to do, but it can also be very healing.

18. You have to choose to find ways to heal. You're the only one who can control what you do with your loss and choose to shoulder your grief and move forward. There may be days where you're lost in the darkness, and that's OK. You just have to choose to get up and try again the next day.

19. Grief often masquerades as fear. Fear alone isn't bad. What is damaging, though, is the inability to move forward in spite of fear. Acknowledge your fear, recognize its legitimacy, and select your path forward. Don't let fear keep you in the darkness.

20. Fear and grief aren't always logical. They're emotions,

and they don't always make sense. You can't rationalize them away.

21. Nothing good comes from thinking about what could have been, should have been, or would have been. The same goes for thoughts like *if only* and *I wish*. None of these can change what happened. They just keep the focus on the loss. Instead, try to focus on the love and memories.

22. Tangible objects can provide comfort. For me, this includes tattoos as beautiful scars for my emotional pain. Pictures may be hard to look at, but they help you remember the person or people you've lost. Your loved ones are more than the loss; photos help you remember the life.

23. Find a purpose for your loss. Nothing will make it OK or better, but a purpose can lighten the load. You can choose to make something good come out of your trauma and loss, even if it's just being there for someone else or trying to understand what they're going through.

24. There is a difference between empathy, sympathy, compassion, and pity. Being pitied was almost unbearable for me. I don't want to be seen as a victim of my circumstances. Instead, I want to be seen as a survivor.

25. Questions such as "Are you married?" or "How many

kids do you have?" may seem innocent at first, but they may not have good answers. These answers will be different depending on how much you want to share or how relevant the question is to the conversation. You may feel guilty if you give the easy answer. If I say that I have two kids, am I "forgetting" Rylee? If I say the boys take after their dad and someone assumes I mean Kyle, am I forsaking Joe? These questions are real, and the answers are real, and there is no wrong answer. The only right answer is the one you feel most comfortable giving at that time.

26. Other questions such as "What would you do if your husband, wife, child, etc. came back?" or "What would you be willing to do to bring them back?" are unfair questions to ask yourself or other people. There is no good answer, because life is so complicated and fluid. Bringing back your loved ones isn't an option, so don't torture yourself by considering it.

27. We are built to grieve. We are built to survive. Even in the darkness, there is life.

Additional Resources Related to Grieving

General Grief Support

- A to Z Healing Toolbox: A Practical Guide for Navigating Grief and Trauma with Intention by Susan Hannifin-MacNab http://www.a2zhealingtoolbox.com/

- Actively Moving Forward (AMF) https://healgrief. org/actively-moving-forward/

- Aircraft Casualty Emotional Support Service (ACCESS) http://accesshelp.org/

- American Association of Retired People (AARP) Grief and Loss Program https://www.aarp.org/home-family/caregiving/grief-and-loss/

- American Association of Suicidology https://suicidology.org/

- American Foundation for Suicide Prevention (AFSP) https://afsp.org/

- Cancer*care* https://www.cancercare.org/

- Center for Loss & Life Transition https://www.centerforloss.com/

- Concerns of Police Survivors (COPS) https://www.concernsofpolicesurvivors.org/

- Daily Strength https://www.dailystrength.org/

- The Dinner Party https://www.thedinnerparty.org/

- Grief Healing https://www.griefhealingblog.com/

- Grief Recovery After a Substance Passing (GRASP) http://grasphelp.org/

- Grief Speaks http://www.griefspeaks.com/

- GriefNet http://www.griefnet.org/

- GriefShare Seminars and Support Groups https://www.grief-share.org/

- Heal Grief https://healgrief.org/

- Healthful Chat https://www.healthfulchat.org/

- Hospice Foundation of America https://hospicefoundation.org/

- Loss of Loved Ones to Sudden Tragedy (LLOST) https://www.llost.org/

- National Fallen Firefighters Foundation https://www.fire-hero.org/

- National Funeral Directors Association Grief Support https://www.nfda.org/consumer-resources/grief-support

- National Hospice and Palliative Care Organization (NHPCO) https://www.nhpco.org/

- Open to Hope https://www.opentohope.com/

- Option B https://optionb.org/

- Our House Grief Support Center https://www.our-house-grief.org/

- Survivors of Suicide (SOS) http://www.survivorsofsuicide.com/

- theravive https://www.theravive.com/

- Tragedy Assistance Program for Survivors (TAPS) https://www.taps.org/

- What's Your Grief? https://whatsyourgrief.com

- Wildland Firefighter Foundation https://wffoundation.org/

Loss of a Spouse

- American Widow Project http://americanwidowproject.org/

- Camp Widow https://campwidow.org/

- Heartache to Healing https://heartachetohealing.com/support-groups-for-widows/

- The Liz Logelin Foundation http://thelizlogelinfoundation.org/

- Sisterhood of Widows https://sisterhoodofwidows.com/

- Soaring Spirits International https://soaringspirits.org/

- Widow Care https://www.widowcare.org/

- Widow Connection http://widowconnection.com/

- Widow Speak http://widow-speak.org/

- Widowed Parent https://widowedparent.org/

- Widowers Organization https://nationalwidowers.org/

Loss of a Child

- Alive Alone http://www.alivealone.org/

- American SIDS Institute https://sids.org/

- BabySteps http://www.babysteps.com/

- Bereaved Parents of the USA https://www.bereavedparentsusa.org/

- Center for Loss in Multiple Births (CLIMB) https://www.climb-support.org/

- The Compassionate Friends: Supporting Family After a Child Dies https://www.compassionatefriends.org/

- Faith's Lodge https://faithslodge.org/

- griefHaven https://griefhaven.org/

- Miscarriage Matters https://www.mymiscarriagematters.org/

- MISS Foundation https://missfoundation.org/

- National Sudden Unexpected Infant Death (SUID) and Sudden Infant Death Syndrome (SIDS) Resource Center https://www.sidscenter.org/

- Now I Lay Me Down to Sleep (NILMDTS) http://www.nowilaymedowntosleep.org/

- Parents of Murdered Children (POMC) http://www.pomc.com/

- Share Pregnancy & Infant Loss Support http://nationalshare.org/

- SIDS Network: A World of Information & Support http://sids-network.org/

- Sudden Unexplained Death in Childhood (SUDC) https://sudc.org/

Loss of a Sibling

- Twinless Twins Support Group https://www.twinlesstwins.org/

For Grieving Children

- Comfort Zone Camp https://comfortzonecamp.org/
- The Dougy Center: The National Center for Grieving Children and Families https://www.dougy.org
- Eluna Resource Center https://elunanetwork.org/
- The National Alliance for Grieving Children (NAGC) https://childrengrieve.org/

For an updated list of resources, including books and podcasts, please visit our website at https://growingwithgrief.com/.

About the Author

AUTUMN TOELLE-JACKSON has lived a life of love and loss, filled with happiness and marked by tragedy. Labels are too simple, but they do have meaning and they do tell part of her story: wife, widow, mother, survivor. The loss of a husband, a beloved cousin and mentor, her daughter, and miscarriages have left scars on her soul and memorial tattoos on her body, but Autumn learned to grow through it all. She found love and reasons to get up each day until those days strung into weeks, then months, then years. This is her story. Autumn and her family created www.GrowingwithGrief.com to provide those who are grieving with a place to find community, resources, and help.